The Art of Reading People:

How to Deal with Toxic People and Manipulation to Avoid (or End) an Abusive Relation

Positive Psychology Coaching Series

Copyright © 2019 by Ian Tuhovsky

Author's blog: www.mindfulnessforsuccess.com

Author's Amazon profile: amazon.com/author/iantuhovsky

Instagram profile: https://instagram.com/mindfulnessforsuccess

All rights reserved. No part of this publication may be reproduced, stored in a retrieval system, or transmitted, in any form or by any means, electronic, mechanical, photocopying, recording or otherwise without the prior written permission of the author and the publishers.

The scanning, uploading, and distribution of this book via the Internet, or via any other means, without the permission of the author is illegal and punishable by law.

Please purchase only authorized electronic editions, and do not participate in or encourage electronic piracy of copyrighted materials.

Important

The book is not intended to provide medical advice or to take the place of medical advice and treatment from your personal physician. Readers are advised to consult their own doctors or other qualified health professionals regarding the treatment of medical conditions. The author shall not be held liable or responsible for any misunderstanding or misuse of the information contained in this book. The information is not indeed to diagnose, treat or cure any disease.

It's important to remember that the author of this book is not a doctor/therapist/medical professional. Only opinions based upon his own personal experiences or research are cited. The author does not offer medical advice or prescribe any treatments. For any health or medical issues – you should be talking to your doctor first.

- INTRODUCTION: A RUDE AWAKENING ... 3
- CHAPTER ONE: THE IMPORTANCE OF READING PEOPLE ... 4
- CHAPTER TWO: THERE ARE NO SAINTS OR VILLAINS ... 9
- CHAPTER THREE: FOCUSING ON QUALITY OVER QUANTITY ... 20
- CHAPTER FOUR: HOW THE BAD GUYS GET IN ... 28
- CHAPTER FIVE: WHY WE HANG ON TO TOXIC RELATIONSHIPS ... 38
- CHAPTER SIX: NARCISSISM AND THE DELUSION OF IMPORTANCE ... 49
- CHAPTER SEVEN: MACHIAVELLIANISM IS NOT JUST PRAGMATISM ... 56
- CHAPTER EIGHT: IT'S ALL ABOUT ME – SOLIPSISM EXPLORED ... 63
- CHAPTER NINE: ANTISOCIAL PERSONALITIES AND SOCIAL ORDER ... 69
- CHAPTER TEN: SHALLOW AFFECT AND EMOTIONAL INTELLIGENCE ... 76
- CHAPTER ELEVEN: "EVIL" - SADISM AND SCHADENFREUDE ... 82
- CHAPTER TWELVE: SPOTTING A PATHOLOGICAL LIAR ... 88
- CHAPTER THIRTEEN: THRILL-SEEKERS ... 97
- CHAPTER FOURTEEN: PSYCHOS, BORDERLINES, CODEPENDENCE - MENTAL HEALTH AND TOXIC RELATIONSHIPS ... 104
- CHAPTER FIFTEEN: ISN'T IT SELFISH TO LOOK OUT FOR MYSELF? ... 112
- CHAPTER SIXTEEN: CULTIVATING OUTCOME INDEPENDENCE ... 118
- CONCLUSION ... 124
- About The Author ... 140

INTRODUCTION: A RUDE AWAKENING

Everyone thinks they're an expert about other people. Maybe even you do. I used to think the same thing for years and years. "I've been dealing with people my whole life, so how could I *not* know how to read people?" Until I reached that stage where life threw me a few hurdles, as it often does, those challenges forced me to reconsider my arrogance, invest in learning, and discover that almost everything I thought I knew might not be true.

See, here's the thing: We can't get better at something until we know our own limits.

We don't really notice how challenged we are at reading people until we do such a bad job we're shocked at ourselves. Which is probably where you are right now. And I know it's hard. I've been there. But you're doing a great thing for yourself: you're taking the first step to truly understanding other people. Not just people who are like you, but people so completely different that until recently you probably never knew they existed.

Fortunately, you don't have to go through it alone. Not only do you have this book as your guide, but, as I did, you will be surprised to find out how many other people are, or have been, in your position. And you will find endless support from them as you begin to learn how to read people.

So even if right now you are still reeling from a painful end to a relationship, do not let that pain consume you. Do not give up on people. In learning to read them, you will learn who isn't on your side and you will also learn who is. You will learn how to avoid bad relationships, but also you will forge great relationships. Which is just as important.

CHAPTER ONE: THE IMPORTANCE OF READING PEOPLE

To understand why it is important to read people, and read them well, we must first know what it means to read people. Let's go to the cliché:

"I read you like a book."

What does that mean? It means that we can see and understand the thoughts and motivations behind their actions as clearly as if they were written down on paper. It means that their secrets are clear to us, like someone is narrating them.

Reading people, also known as social intelligence, involves looking at someone and seeing the deeper meaning behind their actions. We often like to think we are reading people. But in reality, we are usually only guessing. [1]

How do we know we are guessing? Because when we read people "naturally" we're really only empathizing with them. We interpret their emotions and take on their feelings are our own. And then we create our own stories around those feelings. Doing this presents a challenge.

Don't misunderstand, I think empathy is a beautiful thing. Empathy ensures that we look after each other, that we do not cause undue harm, that we show care and consideration even for people outside of our immediate social circle. Empathy is the reason humans make great parents, or that charitable giving and volunteering makes the world a better place.

But empathy can also give rise to solipsism or nihilism. Solipsism means to assume that your reality is the only "real" reality. When you are a solipsist, you act as though everything you perceive, think, and feel is objective. Which means that if someone else perceives, thinks, or

---

[1] Kihlstrom, J. and Cantor, N. (2011) Social Intelligence. *Handbook of intelligence*, 2nd ed. (pp. 359-379). Cambridge, U.K.

feels differently, we judge them as "wrong". [2]

Being a nihilist is a little different. Nihilism denies that there is any distinct "real" or "subjective" reality. When you are a nihilist you act as though anything abstract lacks meaning. A problem arises with that perspective because to us *everyone else's mind* is abstract! We accidentally go back to solipsism. So, our "reality" becomes the rule and we dismiss everyone else's reality as a meaningless bit of abstract thought.

When we try and read people naturally, using empathy, we aren't reading them at all. We are just judging them based on how we would feel, or what we would think if we were in their situation.

This works very well when we are child-rearing or donating to charity. When someone can't tell us what they think and feel, we must use our own thoughts and feelings to gain some perspective. This method also works well when we are interacting with people similar to ourselves.

However, when a person knows us, is in front of us, and is intentionally deceiving us, empathy does not work!

If deception occurs, we need to start being more analytical and start truly reading a person. When we begin reading them, we have to accept that this person may not be who they claim to be. They may be telling lies. Relating fake experiences. Showing fake feelings. Successful reading begins when we unravel their web of lies and get to the real reason behind it.

To actually read someone we need to step outside our own shoes. Because the sort of person who fakes their emotions and lies about what they have experienced and what they think differs from us.

Let's go back to my first experience with a liar. I don't mean a normal person telling a lie,

---

[2] Guillén, J.L. (2013) Why Good People Do Bad Things and What We Can Do About It. *Business Ethics Blog.* IESE.

but someone who consistently, deliberately lied to get their own way. I was around seven or eight at the time, and this other kid at school was always winding me up.

He would call me names, try and hurt me, try and steal my things. And as soon as I reported him to the teachers he masked his expression into the perfect poker face and said he didn't know anything about it. Sometimes he would cry and claim it was *me* who hurt *him*!

I never understood it. Normally when kids fought at school they wanted it resolved as soon as possible. Other bullies I met throughout the years were proud of being bullies. This kid enjoyed hurting me, then lying about it every single time. I could not understand what he got out of it.

I did not know this at the time, but he displayed some strong antisocial traits. Which meant he either had low empathy, or it was suppressed. And I could not understand his behavior because I used empathy to make sense of him. But empathy doesn't work on people without empathy!

Throughout my life, I continued to meet these people. And every time I would try and "naturally read" them using empathy it would never work. Because empathy assumes that the person you are talking to actually feels the same emotion reflected on their face.

People with empathy do sometimes lie, it's true. The difference lies with our intentions. We don't *like* to lie. You can usually tell from looking at someone's face if they are lying or telling the truth. If they are comfortable or uncomfortable. If they are happy or sad.

On the other hand, when you are talking to someone with little or no empathy, then even the emotions on their face are a lie.

When that boy would start crying, at times I would worry he was genuinely upset. But when the teachers left, he stopped. When he claimed to be sorry I thought his face looked honest. Then he did the same thing again.

I couldn't read him because I looked at him the same way I looked at normal kids. And he was not a normal kid.

It took me years and years of meeting people like this before I began to notice something odd about them. Different. It wasn't until an ex-girlfriend accidentally revealed she led a double life that I connected all the dots.

At first, when she spent more time away and money disappeared she would swear it was nothing. Then, when I found out she was stealing money from me to fund shopping sprees, she promised it would never happen again.

Call me a fool, but this happened seven or eight times before I saw the truth. She was lying to my face. She would cry and ask for forgiveness and promise it would never happen again but do it the next day. And one day all the pieces fell into place. She was just like the boy who tried to bully me at school.

After that, it became like shopping for a shiny new red car. You see red cars everywhere when you never noticed them before. I realized that deceptive people were everywhere, doing the same thing, not just to me, but to anyone who let them. Which meant, my ability to read them wasn't as strong as I'd originally thought.

Which brings us back to the central theme of this chapter. Why is it important to read people?

It's important to read people because people lie.

People lie with their words, but also with their actions, and with their expressions. Sometimes people lie for good reasons, or morally ambivalent reasons. We often call these "white lies". Or they may lie for their own selfish gain.

The result of a lie may be good, or neutral, or bad.

We must be honest with ourselves. Can you ever be sure if a lie you've been told is truly helping you? Wouldn't you rather know when someone is lying to you? And wouldn't you like to unravel these lies and enjoy a more genuine experience of the world?

Most of us go out of our way to uncover lies because they make us uncomfortable. Because we would prefer a painful truth.

It's usually not a problem because we can tell when someone is lying and address the issue. When the lie involves someone's thoughts, emotions, or motivations, we're wading out into murky territory. In these situations, we sometimes can't confront the person directly.[3]

Instead, we must observe them, interpret their lies, and adapt.

So how do we even know if someone is lying about a personal issue? Many of us believe that "good" people are honest and "bad" people lie. There's a flaw in that logic as we shall examine in the next chapter:

Do we actually know who the Bad Guys are?

---

[3] Wadley, J. (2013) Manipulative and empathetic people both adept at reading emotions. *Institute For Social Research.* University of Michigan.

CHAPTER TWO: THERE ARE NO SAINTS OR VILLAINS

I know, it sounds pretty counter-intuitive, doesn't it? The problem with the "good person – bad person" dichotomy is that it's really not effective. When we draw a line in the sand and insist everyone on one side is good and everyone on the other is bad, we are turning people into characters. Of course, other people *are* characters, in a way. We cannot see their thoughts or their motivations. So, we project a sort of soap-opera identity onto them, often without even realizing it, so we can explain their behaviors.

"Sandra is a preppy type of a girl, so it makes sense she would be into pop music."

This sort of thinking is okay. It has to be okay, because it is the only way we can get through everyday life. We don't live in anyone's head and we should not pretend to. We sort people into categories and social groups so that we can make sense of what they have done and try and guess at what they will do next. After all, the best predictor of future behavior is past behavior.

The problem arises when we move from characters into "good guys" and "bad guys".

To make sense of our tendency toward categorization, we need to stop thinking of humans as characters and start thinking of humans as complicated social animals.

The first time I did this was completely by accident. I had been talking about an ex-girlfriend to a mutual friend, when he mentioned that her new partner was a real "good guy". My instinctive first thought? "Hey! *I'm* a good guy!" Realizing how insecure and defensive that thought was, I decided to explore it.

Why was I predisposed to think of myself, and people I like, as "good guys"? And why were people I did not get along with and did not like labeled "bad guys"? Before I go on to my own discoveries, I want you to ask yourself the same questions.

What makes a person good?

What makes a person bad?

Who are the good people in your life?

Who are the bad people in your life?

If you are a normal, healthy person, you might find, like I did, that there is a difference between the abstract concept of a "good" person and the people we consider "good" - and likewise where "bad" people are concerned. It is very normal to use big moral arguments, intention, and overall personality when we're talking about people we do not know. But then we use specific incidents and our personal relationship with people to define people we do know.

The problem comes when we define the "good guys" and "bad guys" in our lives in a subjective way, we project all sorts of things onto them. [4]

Take myself versus my ex's new boyfriend. I figured I was the "good guy" and penned her as a "bad guy". Why? Because we had a bad breakup. Does a bad breakup make her actually bad? Of course not. However, it affected my perception of her. And it affected my perception of her new boyfriend. If she was bad, then he had to be a bad too because he was dating her, and they were happy.

If you asked her, how would she identify the bad guy? Who would she identify the good guy? She married the new boyfriend, so I can confidently say that in her eyes, I was the bad guy, and he was the good guy.

And to the rest of the world, like you reading this book, we are just people. We had a bad

---

[4] Guillén, J.L. (2013) Why Good People Do Bad Things and What We Can Do About It. *Business Ethics Blog*. IESE.

breakup. We aren't good or bad.

If you look back on your own negative and positive relationships, you might find that there are some "bad guys" whose only crime is not getting along with you. Yes, there will be some "bad guys" like my school bully, or my shopaholic ex, who can be said to be morally, objectively, bad people. But *most* people we consider bad and good aren't saints or demons, they're just people we clash or click with.

A *huge* part of reading people involves making this distinction!

We can't just treat people we dislike as though they're sociopaths or treat people we like as though they're saints. Because a "bad guy" to us might just be a normal person we don't get along with. A sociopath might be lying to make themselves look charming. That is exactly how normal, healthy, empathetic people get suckered in.

Instead, we need to work on seeing people as objectively as possible. We don't need to do this all the time. What we do need to do is be objective when we read people. For this we need to step back, however briefly, and ask ourselves how a bystander might interpret the situation.

What about the people who are objectively, morally in the wrong, though? Well, we know they are definitely "bad guys" in the conventional sense. A thief or a killer is literally a bad guy. (Whether or not they are to blame for their badness is another debate entirely.) However, when it comes to bad guys who aren't criminals, we also need to ask ourselves whether it's effective to think of them as villains.

Does labeling such people villains, and getting emotionally invested in our relationship with them, help us? I thought of my bully as a villain. It did not help me. I thought of my shopaholic ex as a villain. That did not help me, either.

What would have helped me?

Reading them. Reading them and knowing their intentions could have helped me immensely.

To read people we need to separate ourselves emotionally. We don't need to think of them as villains we need to save the world from. As we shall see, many people lie for various reasons and not all of them are actively hostile. We need to think of them as forces of nature, like a hurricane or a wild dog, for which *we need to be prepared*. And, hopefully, to also prepare others.

If they are criminals or rule-breakers, then we can get rid of them. If we can sever them from our lives - then we should. If we can warn others about their ways and help others to spot, read, and overcome these dangerous people, then we must. If they are unavoidable, then we must learn to prepare for them. We must learn to read them, interpret their tactics, and stop them from hurting us.

Calling them a villain will not prepare us. Reading them will.

Lesson 1: Differentiating between objective and subjective goodness.

As we've discovered together, objective goodness is based on universal moral values. The sort of values so common to humans across the world that they are reflected in law, culture, and societal rules. It is objectively good to not intentionally harm someone else. It is objectively good to stop them from coming to harm.

Objective badness is the mirror opposite of objective goodness. Society punishes objective badness. Harming others is legally defined as abuse. Letting harm come to them when you could stop it is negligent.

Between these two objective definitions lies a moral gray area. For example, a girlfriend who steals your money is objectively bad. A girlfriend who does not steal your money is objectively good. What about a girlfriend who demands your money? Or who asks for money repeatedly?

If she's conscious of her actions and their ramifications, we could argue she is manipulative and harming you intentionally. But if she's ignorant, does that make her good or bad? And how do we tell the difference between the person who demands money because she thinks it's okay, and the one who demands money despite it hurting the giver?

Let's use a more extreme example to drive this point home. Assisted suicide is currently a moral gray area being debated across the world. We know that killing someone is objectively bad, and saving a life is objectively good. But what about helping someone to kill themselves? Some argue that legalizing assisted suicide is just a way of helping those who are suffering. Others say it opens the door for violent people to commit murder.

This debate leads us to an important concept. We cannot tell the willfully abusive and the accidentally abusive apart. We cannot get inside the head of someone who helps their loved one commit suicide and determine if their motivations were good or bad. We can only decide if their *actions* are good or bad. And, if their actions were bad, then we must punish them and prevent them from doing it again.

Likewise, someone who hurts you may be doing it for all the best reasons. Or they might just claim to be helping you. It doesn't matter. If you ask them to stop hurting you and they don't, they are bad for you. [5]

This examination leaves us with four types of people:

1: Those who are objectively good and good for us. These are people who do good things, for the right reasons, and who bring joy and goodness to our lives. We want to surround ourselves with these positive people.

---

[5] Guillén, J.L. (2013) Why Good People Do Bad Things and What We Can Do About It. *Business Ethics Blog*. IESE.

2: Those who are objectively good and bad for us. These are people who do everything for the right reasons or *claim* to do things for the right reasons and we believe them. They are the hardest to break free from because we believe they are inherently good. They may even have the support of others. Their motivation doesn't matter if they are hurting us. We need to ask them to stop. If they don't, we need to start reading.

3: Those who are objectively bad and good for us. These are the second hardest people to break free from because the confuse us about our own intentions. We can see that they are not good people in general, or not good to other people. But their actions benefit us. Which makes it hard for us to break free. In these cases, it is important to read them so that we can protect other people and prepare ourselves for the times when their badness is directed at us.

4: Those who are objectively bad and bad for us. These people don't have much of a place in our lives. We see that they are bad, others say that they are bad, and they do nothing for us. So, unless we've fallen madly in love with the bad-boy/girl, it is very easy to avoid them.

You may notice that with 1 and 4 it is easy to tell these people apart and easy to decide what to do with them. Whereas with 2 and 3 we have a dilemma. 2 is a person who claims to love us while hurting us. As empathetic people, we want to believe them and give them a chance. And 3 is a bad person but there's still something in it for us. Something we want or need. As humans, geared for survival, we cling to bad things that help us, such as soul-sucking jobs, or person 3.

Exercise:

For this exercise, look at the bad people in your life. The ones who either hurt you, or someone you love and trust, that might be considered bad by the above definitions.

Take a blank piece of paper and draw out three columns. "Objectively bad", "Subjectively bad for me", and "Subjectively bad for others".

Sort the bad people in your life into the three columns. Try and be rational and honest. Look at them like you would look at someone you do not know. It can help to use a genuinely bad public figure, such as a criminal, as reference. This way you can be objective.

If a bad person's actions are universally bad, hurt more people than they help, and come from selfish intention, then they are objectively bad.

If a bad person's actions affect you but not others, come from a good or neutral place, or are considered to be accidental or inside a moral gray area, they are subjectively bad for you.

If a bad person's actions affect someone you know, do not hurt most people, come from a good or neutral place, or are considered to be accidental or a moral gray area, they are subjectively bad for others.

After compiling your lists, take some time to think about what makes the objectively bad people different from the subjectively bad people. Think about the why behind their actions. Think about how you could avoid them hurting you or others. It's not enough to make the list. It is important to reflect on the meaning behind this list.

Lesson 2: Playing Devil's Advocate.

When it comes to bad people if you are still having a hard time deciding if they are subjectively or objectively bad, it can help to play Devil's Advocate. A Devil's Advocate is someone who takes something or someone bad and creates a positive argument for them.

This doesn't mean you agree with them!

It involves picking their brains, trying to see what makes them tick. [6]

Thankfully, few people are evil for the sake of evil. Most people are motivated by results. So,

---

6   Davis, J. R. (2013) Improving Students' Critical Thinking and Classroom Engagement by Playing the Devil's Advocate. *Theory, Research, and Action in Urban Education.* CUNY.

if someone is being a bad person, you need to ask yourself how their actions align with their goals.

When we play Devil's Advocate, it can help to focus on four questions.

1) What does this person gain from what they are doing?
2) Does this person know that their behavior is wrong?
3) Does this person change their behavior when corrected?
4) Does this person act selfishly, or with other people in mind?

Just these four questions can explain a lot about people and their motivations.

Usually, when we ask these questions we uncover one of 4 "Bad Guys". And behind these Bad Guys are 4 types of behavior justification. These reasons for the bad behavior are culturally universal, and one of them is always behind harmful actions.

The manipulator. The manipulator wants something, sometimes something physical, from their victims. *Your suffering means nothing as long as they get what they want.* Usually, they want your money, your body, your energy, or your time. Sometimes they want your material goods, or your relationship. The manipulator will either try and take your stuff or will try and ruin what you have. For example: The manipulator wants your money, so they sweet talk you into giving them a loan, which they never repay.

The follower. The follower wants to change you. Sometimes they are compelled by their own idealized version of God. Sometimes by the head of a cult or scam. Sometimes by their parents or friends. *Your suffering is a worthwhile price to pay for the proposed joy you will experience later at the hands of their idol.* This person has a strong, codependent relationship with a powerful manipulator or sadist. So even though the follower often means well, they will do serious harm. For example: The follower believes their preacher can save your soul, so they will hound you to join their faith.

The dreamer. The dreamer has good intentions, but usually falls short of their own goals. There are many reasons for their failure. *Your suffering is purely accidental to them.* When harm is done, they think they can it by doing the same thing again. They think it is their job to fix the mess, or they're genuinely not in touch with reality. For example: The dreamer tried to help you get back together with an old friend, causing everyone heartache. Rather than let things be, they keep trying to set you both up repeatedly.

The sadist. The sadist is the closest we will ever come to evil for evil's sake. They make you suffer, not because your suffering is unimportant, but because *your suffering is deeply important*. Some sadists get a sexual thrill from harming you. Some sadists like feeling empowered and abuse you to feed that urge. Some sadists simply enjoy others suffering like we enjoy a good TV show, something called Schadenfreude. Many healthy sexual sadists engage in consensual sadistic activity with a partner. But plenty of sadists will abuse anyone they can. For example: The sadist saw you drop your keys and kicked them into the drain, for the hell of it.

Two or more of the above. It's important to note that a lot of dangerous people with personality or psychiatric disorders have two, three, or all four of those personality types which makes them particularly bad. Most normal, healthy, morally neutral people will do one or two occasionally. A bad person indulges in one continually. And a dangerous person does two or more continually.

Remember: we can all be any of the four main bad guys at various times and for various reasons.

We might be the manipulator when we lie to get a job. We might be the follower when we nag a friend to come to Church with us. We might be the dreamer when we lose our parents' money on a bad business idea. We might be a sadist when a celebrity we dislike meets some misfortune and we feel joy in their downfall.

These occasional actions are all perfectly normal. All these examples have something else in common. They aren't pathological. They aren't continual. They aren't ruining lives. We do these things once or twice a year like normal, healthy people do. None of us are saints.

Let's explore why a person who regularly acts on two or more of those motivators is dangerous. It's simple: They have a reason. They *always* have a reason. Someone who regularly falls for scams and gives bad advice might not be trying to hurt you. As a dreamer, they will always have a reason to mess up your life. So will someone who gets immense joy from watching you fall and little happiness from anything else. They love hurting you. And that will always be reason enough.

The more reasons someone has to be bad, the more of a Bad Guy they will be.

Exercise:

Look at the people in your life, from people you know, to celebrities and fictional characters, who you consider bad. Ask yourself the four questions.

1) What does this person gain from what they are doing?

Are they being selfish and manipulating you into giving them things? Are they trying to help you? Are they trying to hurt you for their own enjoyment? Why would they want to do this?

2) Does this person know that their behavior is wrong?

Are they malicious? Or do they have their head in the clouds? Do they believe your suffering is meaningless? Do they believe you are not suffering? Do they believe you should suffer?

3) Does this person change their behavior when corrected?

Do they seem remorseful? Do they stop doing the thing you complained about? Do they start doing another hurtful thing? Do they try and make up for the harm they have done?

4) Does this person act selfishly, or with other people in mind?

Are they hurting you because they want to? Because they need to? Or because they think they are helping? Because they are scared? Because they are brainwashed or controlled?

When you determine the answers to these questions, you will conclude whether this person is one of the "Bad Guys". That is, whether they are continually hurting you for one or more reasons. You will also see what type of Bad Guy they are. That is, for what specific reason they are hurting you.

This means you can start playing Devil's Advocate for them.

You do not want to excuse their behavior

You need to explain it.

Devil's Advocacy does this. It takes a person whose actions are harmful and explains them in a light where we can determine their motivation. This puts us in a position where we can avoid being victimized by these people.

Are they trying to control us to feed their power lust? Then we can do things to make them feel less powerful.

Are they assuming their actions are helpful? Then we can set them straight and show them how to actually help.

What's more, by learning their motivations we can also help others. And we can learn to detect similar people in the future. It may be easier to just avoid everyone as soon as they hurt us, but this sort of cagey behavior is not constructive. Reading, and only reading, will help you to spot dangerous people early, maintain relationships with misguided people, and protect yourself and your loved ones from being exploited.

CHAPTER THREE: FOCUSING ON QUALITY OVER QUANTITY

So, what did I mean when I said that cutting out people who hurt us is cagey? Allow me to explain.

Let's go back in time to 2011. I had started a new and exciting business venture with someone I thought was a professional, a visionary with a similar goal to my own, and, above all, a friend.

I was wrong.

We were trying to start a website selling some clothing products. He swore we could get them cheap enough and sell them fast enough to turn a sizeable profit. My contribution involved investing and building the company side. He promised he could handle buying and selling on his own. I invested a lot of time, energy, and money into that idea. It really meant a lot to me, and I was very excited, so I just kept throwing more and more resources at it. And he reassured me. He made me confident that it would work, that it *was* working, and that I would see the results soon. And, as I'm sure you've already guessed, he was lying to me. The venture failed, the business barely afloat, and all my time, energy, and money wasted.

To this day I am still not sure whether he lied on purpose to hurt me, or whether he was caught up in his own delusions. That doesn't really matter right now. What does matter is what I did when I found out.

I cut him off.

The pain of failure and loss overwhelmed me. The only thing I could think of doing to get the turmoil to ebb was to stop talking to him, stop seeing him, end the business venture, and retreat into myself. At first, it provided some relief. I even contemplated quitting business altogether. I wanted to go back to the rat race, just so I never had to suffer like that again.

Which probably sounds ridiculous to you, right? "Why would you give up on business, on independence, on other people and on your dreams because one guy hurt you?" Eventually, I saw the light and understood that I could always try again.

It takes a lot of faith to be that vulnerable again. Even worse, if you never work out what went wrong in the first place then you are putting yourself at risk of repeating past mistakes as soon as you step out there.

For this reason, some people feel like they're magnets for bad relationships. Because in that short window when you're reeling from a bad relationship is exactly when bad people attack. They smell weakness, see the emotional mess that the last bad person left behind, and they swoop in to take advantage of the lessons you haven't had time to learn. So, you get trapped in a cycle of bad experiences and vulnerability until it breaks you. Until you give up.[7]

Nobody ever gives up on people the second or third time they are hurt. Some people keep repeating their actions in an endless loop of the same mistakes while caught in a self-fulfilling prophesy.

Even though it's oftentimes challenging to give people a second chance, it pays to be forgiving if only for your mental and physical health. But remain alert and cautiously optimistic until you know for sure if the person should be avoided.

There are two times in our lives when we give up on people: the first time we are hurt, and the hundredth.

Sometimes people repeat their mistakes for different types of people. The first time a boyfriend hurts them, and the hundredth time a boyfriend hurts them. The first time a friend hurts them and the hundredth time. The first time a coworker hurts them and the hundredth time. But the same principle remains. We either give up at the first hurdle, or when we are so beaten down all our illusions are shattered.

---

[7] HelpGuide.org (2017) Getting Out of An Abusive Relationship.

This is not the best way, for two reasons and I learned that the hard way. Firstly, because the first time is too soon to learn, and the hundredth time is too late to heal. And secondly because *giving up on people is not an option.*

Only one experience isn't conducive to learning and self-growth. If we took the first Bad Guy we ever met and used them to define what Bad Guys are like, we would have some pretty random criteria. "People who wear shorts and like cartoons are jerks." Okay, that was a silly example, but it holds true for other things as well. Some of us may have experienced a lying Bad Guy. Others may have experienced a brutally honest Bad Guy. Both can still be Bad Guys, through and through. We just can't work out what makes someone bad from that first experience. The only option is to try again.

The hundredth time is too late to heal because we have been betrayed too many times. Once you have experienced a few Bad Guys you need to start thinking about what makes them tick. As mentioned, this sort of person is an opportunist. A Bad Guy always looks for an opening, and if you just lost a Bad Guy then the next one that moseys along will assume you're hiring. And they're not "Bad Guys" for nothing. This sort of person will abuse you mentally, physically, financially, emotionally, socially, etc. If you wait too long to connect the dots, they will have taken everything you have.

That being said, we shouldn't give up on people because of one bad apple, or one type of personality. People are wonderful. You are a person and you are nothing like the Bad Guys you've known. There are probably have many people you know and love, or admire. And they're not Bad Guys. Later, we will see some exact statistics. For now, rest assured. Bad Guys are the minority!

Is that to say we should never evict bad people from our lives? Of course not! Some people will do us some serious harm and we need them gone.

It is imperative to remember that it's worth keeping people around if:
- they make each other happy,

- they add value to each other's lives, or
- there is still more to learn from them.

Almost every person you encounter will meet some or all of the above criteria! And when a person stops adding value to your life, a healthy relationship moves apart organically, without you needing to block their number.

So, a few people are worth avoiding entirely, but most people we meet will play some part in our lives, and most relationships end in a natural and healthy way.

After completely understanding the criteria above, we hit another issue: There are more types of person than just "avoid" and "friend".

We all know this, of course. But it gets increasingly difficult to draw the boundaries, especially with the development of social media, social movements, and "friendly" marketing. Everyone claims to be our friend. Then we find it hard to determine who our real friends are.

When you think about your friends, do you think about social media friends? People you know from high-school? People you see at least once a week? People who would help you out in a pinch? People you can trust with your secrets?

Any of them can be friends. But none of those characteristics make them your friend. Not being a friend doesn't mean they are an enemy. They are just somewhere between acquaintance and a friend. Which is a fine place to be.

The problem is that we are losing our concept of social circles. In the past we used to think of "inner circles" and "outer circles". Our "inner circle" would be people who:

- we know closely,
- we trust intimately,
- we enjoy spending time with, whether it's daily or once a year,

- we help each other mutually,
- we are equivalent, if not equals,
- would be there for us if we needed something badly,
- would stand by our side through hard times, and
- would not mind telling us to our face when we are wrong.

People can be lovely, fun, worthwhile people without meeting all these requirements. However, they would not be friends. They would be people in our outer circle.

We, as a society, are reaching a point where we consider our acquaintances, our employers, and our idols to be our friends, when they obviously cannot be. A lot of this pressure to consider everyone your friend comes from the manipulators of society. They want us to consider them our friends because they want our time, energy, and money. That is why people beg for approval on social media via likes, shares and other post engagement. That is why brands call their customers "friends" or "family". That is why some people expect us to treat them, no matter how well we know them, with respect and admiration.

We need to adjust our perspective. Because right now most of us are giving them what they want. Even I do sometimes. People-pleasing is not a habit you break, but an influence. You need to always look out for it.

Why? Because your time, energy, and money are limited.

You only have so much time on this planet.

You only have so much energy to spare.

Your money, a representation of the time and energy you put into your work, is also limited.

Not everyone can be your friend, because there are only so many people you can be a meaningful and genuine friend to.

What does this mean in practical terms? It means we must stop worrying about the number of our friends and start worrying about the quality of our relationships. Which is easier said than done.

Quantity of friends refers both to our number of friends, and to who is our friend. We don't want or need everyone to be our friend. It just isn't possible. Some people will think you are okay. Some people will think poorly of you for no reason. Some people cannot be a friend to you, because they cannot know you, treat you as an equal, or give you their time. There's nothing wrong with that, so don't take it personally. It's just normal, human behavior.

When we focus too much on the quantity of friends we have, on how many friends we have and who is and isn't our friend, we take our present friends for granted. Which means we neglect them. We can't not. We assume that we need to put our limited time and energy into getting more people to like us, and specific people to like us. And that will never work. Because most of the time these people whose attention we want will not be our friends. Even when they *do* become our friends, we will stop giving them our time and energy, because we will be chasing a new friend.

Instead, we need to focus on the quality of our relationships. The quality of a relationship is not based on how important the other person is to society. Or on how much time we spend together. It is based on how enjoyable we find each other's company. The highest quality friends will be the ones with whom we can share treasured, intimate moments without hiding our true self. These are the people we need in our inner circle. These are the people who must get our time and energy.

Lesson 3: Culling the herd.

When we first try and determine who our friends are, it is easy to get defensive. Let's face the facts, it's hard for us to drop from 300+ "friends" to only 1-12 friends. For that reason, it is necessary to have a little perspective.

Robin Dunbar, a professor at Oxford, has studied human relationships extensively. You may know him from the "Dunbar numbers". His conclusion reflects that we can only have a stable relationship with 150 people at most.

Through his research he defined that we can only be truly intimate with 5 people. These people define our lives and our identities. We spend the most time with them and cherish them the most.

The next closest layer, which we could consider a family of sorts, rises to 15 people. These extra 10 include people close to us, but who probably do not know all our secrets and who we would not necessarily seek out in a crisis.

Then we have the next 50 people. The extra 35 include people we like and go out of our way to spend time with, but are not intimate with, emotionally, mentally, or physically.

Finally, we have the biggest group, of 150 people. The final 100 provide a positive influence in our lives, but maybe are people we have very little to do with most of the time.

Everyone else? They are not good people or bad people. They are just acquaintances. We do not have enough time and energy to have a meaningful impact on each other's lives. Were we or them to vanish from the face of the earth, either could be replaced effortlessly. [8]

We need to understand this. Not because everyone outside the 150 is completely superfluous. They are necessary, important, valuable human beings. However, they are not our friends, and we should not give them first priority of our very limited time and energy.

Lesson 4: Protecting the inner circle.

---

[8] Dunbar, R. (1998). Grooming, gossip, and the evolution of language (1st Harvard University Press paperback ed.). Cambridge, Mass.: Harvard University Press.

How does this information tie into reading people? It is relevant because if we do not have a true understanding of who our friends are, anyone can infiltrate our inner circle. And this is dangerous, not just to us, but to everyone inside the circle. When a Bad Guy gets in, our friends and families are at as much risk as we are.

Our inner circle exists in some form, even if we do not see it or feed it. There are always people who consider us their nearest and dearest. People who trust us implicitly. People who truly love and respect us. When we add someone new to our friendships, our inner circle trusts this person also.

If that person is a good, normal person (which most of the time they will be), then there is no problem. But if that person has bad intentions, then we have just given them free rein to hurt not only us, but everyone we love and respect!

If we become cagey and shut other people out for good, we will not let any Bad Guys into our inner circle. This also restricts everyone else. Those countless perfectly good, normal people who could add immense value to our lives, and us to theirs.

The solution? To identify and define our inner and outer circles. When we know the identity of everyone within our inner and outer circles, we can stop people from advancing too quickly from our outer circle inwards, and protect the most important people in our lives.

Exercise:

For this exercise, make an effort to picture your inner circle. Bear in mind you are not picking the people you would like to have in your inner circle. All of us have a celebrity or two who we would include if we could!

I need you instead to look at who *actually* meets the criteria for a true friend. Who in your life is truly there for you, and you for them? Don't feel ashamed if there are only four or five people, or even one person, who is a true friend. This is normal. Despite the slant of the media, that is the number of close friends you can realistically be a friend to.

CHAPTER FOUR: HOW THE BAD GUYS GET IN

Everything we've discussed will only help you deal with the Bad Guys who are already in your social circles. Hopefully, they haven't wormed their way into your inner circle already. They won't if you keep a close eye on the quality of your inner circle and who is in it. But they are still in one of your social circles. So... how did they get that far, anyway?

A good part of the mystery can be explained away with the work we completed in Chapter Three. We just aren't guarding our social circles, so our outer circles are pretty much a revolving door of almost everyone we know at any given point. This makes it very easy for someone completely unknown to us to become an acquaintance, then a friend, then a close friend, in a matter of weeks.

But that's not the whole story. Because however open and friendly your social circles are, and however unguarded you are about letting people in, it takes two to tango. The Bad Guy had to want to get into your social circle, too. Which is a bit more complicated to explain. And which actually takes us back to our moral matter from Chapter Two: There Are No Saints Or Villains.

Quite simply, a social circle is a desirable place to be. Humans are social animals. We cannot do everything we need to in order to survive all on our own. So, we have evolved to enjoy the company of other people. These two components are at the core of all our social interactions. We either relate with people useful to us, or people we like. Our relationship with a bank teller, or a cashier is important to us on a survival level, but not on an emotional one. Our relationship with our faith or our sports team is important to us on an emotional level, but not a survival one. Both of these relationships are completely outside our circles. The most important relationships, such as those we have with family members, friends, and partners, are important both for survival and emotional well-being.

To be physically safe and emotionally fulfilled are the only reasons a person seeks a relationship with another human being. Unfortunately, they're also the reasons why a Bad Guy wants a relationship.

Bad Guys are humans, too, with the same instinct to survive and the same need for human contact. A Bad Guy doesn't always join your social circle with the express purpose of hurting you. A Bad Guy joins your social circle because they want something from you. There are several key differences between how a friend behaves and how a Bad Guy behaves within your social circle.

First of all, a bad guy does not classify people's closeness based on that combination of usefulness and emotional well-being which we discussed. Many people confuse this blasé attitude as Bad Guys lacking emotional needs.

Secondly, a Bad Guy hurts you. It is vitally important to remember the distinction.

Finally, a Bad Guy, for these reasons, places no true value on belonging to your social circle. To a Bad Guy, the degree of closeness they share with a person does not matter. It is only the *number* of social circles they belong to which is important to them.

There's really little difference between your reasons for relating to someone, and a Bad Guy's reasons. You might say that a Bad Guy will use you for sex, or money, or free labor. But so will a wife, a friend, and a relative. In all these scenarios, you are willingly giving. You might say that a Bad Guy sets out to hurt you, but they do not. Your pain is just incidental. They would do this whether it hurt you or whether it did not.

The three main social differences between Bad Guys and the rest of us are as follows. First, the bad guy does not value you intrinsically. Second, the Bad Guy harms you. Last, the Bad Guy collects social circles. Beyond that, any one of us or our friends could possess *individual Bad Guy traits*, which does not make us a Bad Guy any more than having a symptom of autism makes us autistic.

I suppose you are now thinking to yourself, "Well, this theory is all well and good, but how does it play out in the real world?" I'm glad you asked! We can actually see examples of the Bad Guys breaking into social circles every day, and sometimes, if we look closely, we can capture a glimpse of their true motivations, as well as of the three social differences between them and us.

For the remainder of this chapter we will explore some concepts related to how Bad Guys break into our social circles, illustrated with examples from my own life. These strategies are not all used by all Bad Guys, or exclusively by Bad Guys. They are not unique to any type of Bad Guy, either. And not all Bad Guys are even aware of their own bad behavior since it comes naturally to them. And all Bad Guys will use one or more of the following strategies to weasel their way in to social circles.

Recruiting and Applying.

When I still worked for a small marketing firm, I had a coworker who seemed obsessed with me. Literally everything I did, she would want to be involved. Every time I said something she would speak up. Every time I needed something she would rush to help. Every time she needed something she would ask me. At first, I figured, "Hey, this lady really, really likes me."

Then she started recruiting. She had wormed her way into the outermost reaches of my social circles. Rather than settle there, or try and push ahead, she wanted to drag me out and into *her* social circles. She would do this by continually placing demands on me. By trying to pick away at my work relationships, spreading rumors, etc. By generally making me feel unstable and trying to make me feel like I needed her.

When someone is recruiting, they are trying to persuade you to join them. They want you to lean on them heavily, to rely on them. So, they start out with a very mutual relationship, but then they slowly coerce you to do more and more. As time goes by you will find you're doing everything for them. They have used that time to separate you from your friends and/or coworkers, so you find it difficult to push the recruiter away. They are the only person left to help you, even if you work for 5 hours to get 5 minutes of their time.

The process of applying is a little more insidious because it is harder to work out what the person is doing until it is too late. A recruiter picks away at your relationships and draws you into their social circle, but an applier just keeps moving into your social circles, pushing everyone else out. The end result is the same, but because it is not as harsh as recruiting, you might miss it.

Both recruiting and applying work because we actually like the people we help. It's a weird quirk of humans, but when we feel someone is indebted to us we feel they are more trustworthy and better people. On the other hand, when we feel indebted to others, we work hard to re-balance the scales. This strategy works great for normal people with empathy. But when a Bad Guy figures this out, they will help us, convincing us to help them, and then slowly withdraw their support. Which ends up with us doing everything for them, them not having to provide anything to the relationship, and us liking them for it! [9]

Trauma Bonding.

One time at scout camp, I developed a pretty weird friendship with this older kid. For some reason he would really pick on me. Not just like normal boys being a bit mean to each other, or bantering. Really mean. Pushing me over, pulling my hair, stealing my pudding, calling me names, and blaming me for *his* actions. I remember feeling hurt and confused that someone I had only just met would hurt me so much.

And yet he remained my friend. Because after all that, at the end of the day, he would present a peace offering. If he pushed me over and I was bleeding from my knees, he would get the first aid kit. If I became withdrawn after an insult, he would reassure me. If I took the fall for something he did, he would offer me candy from his stash. At the time, I felt this was okay and normal. I guessed he was just a bit rough naturally, but that he meant well and that, deep down, *he really was my friend.*

And the second I stopped being a victim? He would resume his abuse multiplied by ten. If ever I told anyone he would call me a pussy, a weakling, and a tattle-tale. If I insulted him back his insults escalate, or he would get physical. If I didn't act hurt or cry he would refuse to offer me kind words or comfort. Little did I know it at the time, but this kid was *not* my friend. He was conditioning me to rely on him. Which I did until the end of the camp. After

---

[9] Whitbourne, S. K. (2012) Don't Be Fooled by a Narcissist. *Psychology Today.* PsychologyToday.com

the camp, when we parted ways, he just wouldn't talk to me, wouldn't even offer his phone number. He was done picking on me and went home to find a better victim.

Trauma bonding is an interesting phenomenon. The idea is that people in difficult situations will unite for safety in numbers. Even if that difficult situation was caused by one of the people in the group! By causing trauma our Bad Guys put us in a position where we are open to bonding. By providing relief from the trauma they become at once the poison and the medicine.

This goes a long way toward explaining physically and emotionally abusive relationships, and why these harmful relationships often affect people from lower socioeconomic groups and troubled backgrounds. It is easier for the Bad Guy to start out offering refuge from pre-existing trauma than to create the trauma in the first place. That way they enter the cycle more easily and are not detected.[10]

Love Bombing.

In college I had what one could fairly consider a toxic girlfriend. Yet she was also, at first, a woman many guys would consider the ideal girlfriend. As soon as we met we clicked, and amazingly well. She was hot, although I would like to think I was hot, too. She was witty and funny. A little rude but I found her honesty refreshing. We started going out and our connection only seemed to be getting stronger. She would buy me gifts, pay my half of the bill, and call me and message me all day long, telling me how hot I was and how much she loved me and missed me. We would talk for hours and hours about everything, from celebrities to deep philosophical thoughts. I gave her my keys and would come home to someone waiting for me.

She was totally the one, right? At the time, as an immature boy, I thought so, too.

All this changed as soon as we moved in together. Literally, it was like turning off the light and not knowing what just happened. As soon as her last box was in my apartment, she

---

[10] Christman, J. A. (2009) Expanding the Theory of Traumatic Bonding as it Relates to Forgiveness, Romantic Attachment, and Intention to Return. *Trace: Tennessee Research and Creative Exchange.* University of Tennessee.

would demand money from me, never had time for sex, never wanted to talk or do things together, and continually put me down while giving me the silent treatment over trivial things.

At first, I was terrified I'd done something wrong. After all, this lovely, charming woman who really, truly loved me was suddenly... terrible to me. I bent over backwards trying to help her. I did everything she asked. I pandered to her emotionally and never retaliated when she hurled her anger in my direction. After trying to work it out, eventually I realized that either I had been duped, or we'd simply grown too far apart to ever close the gap.

As an adult, I now kick myself for ever falling for Love bombing since it's a Bad Guy tactic that can possibly be avoided with a little awareness. Love Bombing works with young people, passionate people, and vulnerable people. When you are riding that high of a new friendship, and especially of a new romance, your feelings seem to be reflected in the other person. You want to give them the moon, so when they want to give you the moon, too, it can feel like true love. We believe it because we think they're experiencing the same extreme emotions.

The problem with love bombing is that eventually it stops. Not like the slow burn out of romantic passion which can and does happen to us all. It crashes and burns like a sudden stopping of affection, literally overnight. Because the love bomber's emotions were not real. Their "bombs" of love were just elaborate displays to convince us that they were invested in the relationship. That way they could persuade us to let go, get emotional, and sacrifice ourselves for them. They gain our trust, and with it access to our energy, time, money, friends, etc.

So eventually this false love ends. This will happen during one of two scenarios. It will stops suddenly because the victim gets wise to it. Either they have experienced love bombing before or seen it happen to someone close to them. They simply don't fall for it. Just like that, this person who adored them and would do anything for them is suddenly in love with someone else.

Love bombing also usually ends when they get what they want. Eventually, the Bad Guy will charm someone into falling passionately in love with them who is vulnerable and needy, who is young and inexperienced, or simply who lives life to the fullest. These people are very likely to fall for love bombing. And as soon as the Bad Guy has the victim where they want them, the love bombing stops. Sometimes the relationship ends, and the Bad Guy vanishes again. All too often the victim desperately tries to appease the Bad Guy, to get the relationship back.

Love bombing works because it appeals to the fallacy of sunk costs, the part of our brain which believes that if we have already invested something, we should keep investing. The same principal that keeps people gambling will keep people working for a relationship which is already gone.[11]

Mirroring.

Thinking back to my old business partner who disappointed me, I recall how he gained my trust. When we first met, he seemed a little awkward, a little shy, a little quiet. I never minded this, because I like introverts. I never thought there could be something else lurking underneath the shy exterior. Over time, as he began to open up to me, it turned out we had a lot in common. The same moral values, the same goals, the same ideals. When I talked about something I was passionate about, he would respond with the same passion. So, I figured that he would make the perfect business partner. After all, we were headed in the same direction, right?

Only we couldn't have been. Because even though he claimed that lies offended him, he lied to me repeatedly. Even though he claimed to be into fashion and to know how to access cheap products for resale, he actually knew very little about it. It was all fake. I have no idea who this guy really was, but he wasn't like me.

Mirroring is an enormously successful strategy Bad Guys use which we often have a hard time seeing until it hits us. I still fall for the early stages of mirroring to this day, and it can take me a couple of days of knowing someone before I finally read them well enough to spot their mirroring!

---

[11] Strutzenberg, C. (2016) Love-Bombing: A Narcissistic Approach to Relationship Formation. UARK.

When a Bad Guy mirrors us, they generally pose as a shy introvert at first. This is so that they can't say or do anything which could offend you, or make you feel they are different from you. They use this time to watch you, listen to you, and learn about you. When it happened to me social media was not a big part of my life, so this guy must have been very good at reading people to figure me out. Now, when everyone has a digital paper trail, even the dumbest of Bad Guys could meet you, go home, and learn a lot about you overnight.

Once they know enough about us, they will pretend to discover it. They will drop a mention of a musical artist they know we like and have probably listened to their most and least popular songs, so we're delighted by their expertise. They will claim to like the uncommon and unique things about us, forging an unlikely bond, such as saying, "I know most people do not like horses, but I think they are fab." Bad Guys do this to create a sensation of "Us VS The World", like they are our soulmates and no one else cares enough and is qualified enough to help us.

This strategy encourages us to overthrow our usual social norms and fast-track the Bad Guy into our inner circle. Someone we have only known a few weeks suddenly becomes worth dating. Someone whose credit history we do not know is a business partner. We take our new BFF's word over our own mother's. Because we are like them, and they are like us, and that is rare and special. Only it's all a lie. They are not like us, and the ways in which they are like us probably aren't all that rare.

Mirroring works so well as a strategy precisely because the people who pull it off are great liars, and the bad liars who attempt it just come across as insecure people who want to please us. Quite simply, there is no way for a Bad Guy to fail when they use this strategy. Well, except for when we read them.[12]

Lesson 5: Identifying attempts at infiltrating.

---

[12] Spaeth, D. (2014) The Two-Way Mirror: Projection, Responsibility, and Connection. Saybrook University.

Identifying when someone is genuinely interested in getting to know us or when someone is just trying their luck to see if they can exploit us is not an easy task. In the moment, we tend to give people the benefit of doubt. Which is normally a good thing. But if we do not learn what an attempt at infiltrating looks like, then it will happen to us repeatedly.

For that reason, it is better to look back on our own experiences and try and get a real feel for spotting infiltration attempts. We can study martial arts theory and still be a terrible fighter. We can study cooking theory and be a terrible chef. We can study the tactics of manipulative people and still get manipulated.

On the flip side, someone who has never read this book, or any on psychology, but who has lived with manipulative people their whole life can often see an infiltration attempt from a mile away. They have that hands-on experience.

We want to fall somewhere in the middle. We don't want to be completely book-taught, as theory does not match up to experience. We do not want to suffer repeatedly at the hands of Bad Guys just to learn a life lesson. Which is why we need to make the time to really reflect on our lives and analyze the actions of the Bad Guys in our pasts. That way, we get a little theory, a little experience, and mash them together into something useful.

In doing so, we are proactively protecting ourselves, and our loved ones, from Bad Guys who want to gain our trust and exploit us.

Exercise:

Look back at times when someone truly manipulative has entered your life. Think back to the things they said and did. Try and see if these examples fit into any of the four main strategies. A Bad Guy will rarely combine strategies, as doing so would be unsuccessful. Instead, they stick to one path and will relentlessly use it until it either succeeds, or you chase them away.

If you generally keep manipulative people at bay, ask yourself how and why you do this. Maybe your instincts are really finely tuned, but if you aren't doing this consciously, then you are still vulnerable. Write down the things that make you aware of a Bad Guy, the things that put you on your guard.

By analyzing how these different Bad Guy infiltration strategies take shape in the real world, you will be better prepared to actually face off with one of these people.

CHAPTER FIVE: WHY WE HANG ON TO TOXIC RELATIONSHIPS

A toxic relationship is, as you have probably already guessed, a relationship with a Bad Guy.

Many of us assume that only romantic relationships can be toxic, but the reality is that *any* relationship can be toxic if we let it. For example, my scout camp bully/friend was a great example of a toxic friendship, and my business partner was a great example of a toxic professional relationship. Any time that you experience a Bad Guy's desire to trample you for their own gain, the relationship is toxic. No matter the situation or the level of abuse.

It's important to remember that last part. Yes, it is possible to have a toxic relationship with a teacher or coworker. Yes, it is possible to have a toxic relationship where the abuse is subtle and psychological. And these relationships can be as harmful as a toxic romantic relationship with someone who is physically abusive. In some cases, they can be more harmful, as we are more willing to accept abuse when it comes in an unexpected form from an unexpected person.[13]

So, for the record, you can have a toxic relationship that is between:

- romantic partners
- parent and child
- friends
- coworkers
- boss and employee
- teacher and student
- a group and an individual

Those relationships can be toxic either way. That is to say, either party could be the Bad Guy. And those relationships could hurt you:

---

[13] Lake Effects Blog. (2014) How to Identify and Diffuse Toxic Work Relationships. Lake Forest Graduate School of Management.

- physically
- mentally
- emotionally
- spiritually

Your experience of abuse and toxic relationships *is no less valid* than the experiences of someone who was in a more stereotypical toxic relationship. The hurt suffered in these relationships is real. The scars are real. You still need time to heal from it all.

That said, usually, as soon as we notice that a relationship is toxic, we start moving away. There is an instinct in us that says, "This person is dangerous, so let's go." When we see someone who isn't leaving a toxic relationship, it is easy to assume they don't have it so bad. Or, when we know how bad they have it, we find it hard to understand why they stay.

Everyone who deals with Bad Guys gets asked this question: Why do you stay?

Domestic violence survivors and their advocates are often asked, "why do you stay with an abusive partner?" Bullied kids are asked, "why do you still hang out with them?" Cult survivors are asked "how could you let it go so far?" The assumption is that there is a certain threshold after which we should and will just back out. The assumption says, "If that were me, I would have left ages ago!" This assumption doesn't only hurt survivors, but it hurts us, too.

It boomerangs back to us because when we assume these things cannot happen to us, we are totally unprepared when they do. We are all at risk of getting trapped in a toxic relationship. Even Bad Guys get trapped by other Bad Guys or get into mutually toxic relationships! The only way we can escape this problem is by learning how to read and become active participants in analyzing our own relationships.

However, when we are the person hanging onto a toxic relationship we are too deep in it to be rational, utilizing all the justification we have at our disposal.

"They aren't really like that."

"I don't have another option."

"They never hit me."

"It's the community aspect I'd miss."

"I don't want to hurt them."

"They offer me something amazing, something I can't find anywhere else."

"I take the good days with the bad."

"It's not their fault, they are just mentally ill."

"I have to think of others before myself."

All these reasons would be acceptable if we were referring to a minor character flaw in the Bad Guy, like being too loud, or forgetful. When we are talking about *abuse*, these reasons become euphemisms, to hide the real reasons we stay because the real reasons for holding on to toxic relationships are not comfortable to face. But we must face them if we want to escape the Bad Guys.

There are three reasons we hold on to toxic relationships: an insecure future, extreme attraction, and fear. These three reasons explain our actions, and even our excuses. When we say, "I take the good days with the bad", we are actually saying we have an extreme attraction to the Bad Guy. This really means we will put up with the bad days just to get a taste of the good days. When we say, "I don't have another option", we are actually saying that our other options are terrifying to us.

By using euphemisms to hide from the three core reasons, we soothe our emotional wounds. It's a bit like putting a bandage over a broken bone. The bone will not heal unless we give it proper treatment. And in order to offer that treatment, we need to unroll the bandages and assess the damage. It will not be a pretty sight. However, it will help us in the long run. [14]

Insecurity plays the biggest part in why we nurture a toxic relationship. Insecurity takes many forms. For example, we could be insecure in ourselves and be seeking validation and support from our Bad Guy. We could stay in a relationship with a Bad Guy because we feel the future without them would be too uncertain.

Insecurity like this comes about because humans are creatures of habit and comfort. We get into a routine and we hate changing it. This, in terms of evolution, really makes sense. If we were living in one place where there was food and water, even if there were frequent storms, it would make sense to stay there so long as there was still food and water. It is comfortable and easy to stay. On the other hand, leaving the stormy area might mean we could not find food or water on time, and could die.

Here's the problem with this philosophy. We are not cavemen settling in a bad area because we have no options. Our primitive subconscious doesn't know this. Our evolved, conscious mind *does*. We have options. We can and will survive. No matter how comfortable you are, remember that you can become comfortable again, but without a toxic relationship. You might lose a partner, a relative, a job, or a friend. But you will gain a life. Is that not worth it?

I was definitely in an insecure place after my two Bad Guy ex-girlfriends. Both played into my insecurities about my role as a boyfriend, and my insecurities about being alone. The girl who kept taking my money and going on shopping sprees made it feel like this was a small mistake, not intentional harm. The girl who went cold and distant relied on the fact we'd already moved in together. They both needed me to think that it would be too much effort

---

[14] Christman, J. A. (2009) Expanding the Theory of Traumatic Bonding as it Relates to Forgiveness, Romantic Attachment, and Intention to Return. *Trace: Tennessee Research and Creative Exchange.* University of Tennessee.

to end the relationship. At first, I did.

And what happened when I broke up with them? Sure, my comfortable routine disappeared for a bit. But so did the treatment. Which left me to form a new routine more in line with my personal values.

Extreme attraction is also essential to persevering in a toxic relationship. You know the saying "Love is blind", right? What that means is that extreme attraction makes us overlook things we might normally consider deal breakers, either for personal reasons or because of our culture or background. And this is normally a good thing. Again, when two people with empathy are blindly in love, or when one person with empathy is blindly in platonic love with another person with empathy, nobody is abused. Feelings may get hurt. You may be disappointed when you fall out of love. You love as long as love lasts, and even if it ends, you move on.

It is easy to forget that extreme attraction can be exploited. Sure, extreme attraction can blind you to someone's burn scars, or class, or depression, and that is a beautiful thing. That said, extreme attraction can also blind you to someone's abusive tendencies, lack of empathy, and desire to exploit you. Which means that we can sit there, all loved up, while someone, for example, stops being the person we used to love. Love, simply put, makes us vulnerable to manipulation.

Another thing we neglect about extreme attraction is that it is not just sexual. Think about how fiercely many people defend their family, best friend, or favorite artist. When something is very, very important to us, we experience extreme attraction, whether or not we are sexually attracted to that person or thing. We are just as vulnerable to exploitation from, say, a brother, or a religious leader, as we are to exploitation from a partner.

So why is this even a thing? It turns out, extreme attraction serves a biological function.

Extreme attraction is our body's way of compromising. Nothing and nobody is perfect, that much we know. So, what happens when someone we need to support, like our child, has a trait we find undesirable, such as lying? Or a person who is very sexually compatible with us has a trait we used to consider a deal breaker? Or a person who would be a great business partner speaks in a way we can't tolerate? In these cases, our love blinds us to their "imperfections", promoting survival. This helps us form connections despite bad experiences and prejudices which would otherwise stop us from relating to others.

A great example of both extreme attraction that was not sexual, and of the negative effects of extreme attraction, was my connection to my former business partner. I was so loved up with the idea of the business, so convinced it was a wonderful thing, that I was blinded to his inexperience and lies. I wanted it to work too badly. And when it didn't, I daresay I felt a little heartbreak.

Fear is the final component to the survival of a toxic relationship. Even if they do not directly threaten you, a Bad Guy knows full well that you are afraid and definitely exploits that fear. Bad Guys need you to be afraid, of them or of something else, to use you.

Fear is a very healthy thing to have. Indeed, being truly fearless would put us in danger. We should definitely be afraid of falling from great heights, growling dogs, and of leaving our homes unattended. These fears are nature's way of telling you when something threatens your survival, sort of like a memo saying, "Hey, you're mortal, so take care!"

But fear can be manipulated for nefarious purposes. We already explored one kind of fear when we talked about insecurity concerning the future. In that case, we are afraid of uncertainty, of what will happen if things change, or of losing our routine. There are many fears which keep us in toxic relationships.

There is the fear of the other person, their violent tendencies or what they are capable of doing as an act of revenge. This fear is the one most of us think of when we consider an abusive relationship. Fear they will hurt you. Stalk you. Turn your friends against you. Outside of romance, you may fear losing your job, being hurt, or having to move away.

There is the fear of social stigma. This one is a bit like the fear of revenge, except it is not explicit. Nobody walked up to you and said, "you will be shunned forever if you end that relationship". You just know, from external influences and seeing it happen to others, that ending the relationship is not acceptable to some people in your culture.

There is the fallacy of sunk costs. This is again part of the insecurity package. You say, "I have already given X dollars, Y hours, and Z energy to this person, so I need to continue, or it will all be a waste!" The assumption is that if you keep going, eventually your investments will pay back. But toxic relationships are stock that never regains its value. And, worst of all, the more you invest, the more committed you are to investing! It's a dangerous cycle.

There are other fears which may keep people together, such as the fear of harming children, the fear of missing out on a reward, etc., but these tend to be personal, and are not present in all toxic relationships. On the other hand, the fears of losing connections, revenge, stigma, and sunk costs, are very common and usually one or more of them is responsible for holding a toxic relationship together.

In all my toxic relationships, I have been afraid to lose the connection more than anything. I felt that these people genuinely valued me, and I was scared that I would be nothing without their love and support. That love and support was not real! I also at times feared the sunk costs. I figured I had given so much money, time, and energy, that I had to stick around to get it all back. I never got it back. I just ended up losing more money, time, and energy.

So, as you can see, there are many reasons why we may cling onto a toxic relationship, but all of them fit, in some way or another, into one or more of those three categories. Deep down, those are our three main reasons.

Lesson 6: Identifying excuses.

Identifying our own excuses can be hard. The difficulty comes in because the three reasons for holding on to a toxic relationship can manifest in many different ways. It all depends on who we are, who they are, the nature of our relationship, how long we have been together, etc. If you are in a toxic relationship, your reasons for staying are probably excuses, and will certainly echo back to insecurity, extreme attraction, and fear.

For example, let's take some of the excuses at the start of this chapter:

"They aren't really like that."

Here we are expressing that the other person, most of the time, is completely different than how they appear, which may be true. But if you are in an abusive relationship, this sentence *covers for the other person*. We are telling a lie to protect them which is coming from a place of fear. What are we afraid of? Perhaps we fear their physical or psychological violence. Perhaps we fear the social stigma of being discovered to be in a toxic relationship. Whatever our motivation, hiding someone else's bad actions comes from a place of fear.

The sentence above also provides an excuse for their bad behavior. Just because they aren't normally like that, does it excuse their actions? Perhaps if you followed it up by saying, "their mother died earlier this week", they could be excused. And yet, if they are doing this without a valid reason, or because of a hair-trigger temper, they should not be excused. In that situation, we are seeing extreme attraction. We are saying, "because they act in another way most of the time, it is okay for them to act this way some of the time."

"I don't have another option."

Here the overarching reason is insecurity. There are always options. What we mean to say in this situation is that we fear our options. Maybe the option is undesirable. For example, being forced to live on the streets, or hunt for a new job in a weak employment market. Maybe the option is uncertain, such as finding a new partner. Abusive people tend to try their hardest to take away our options and make us flail without them, creating a strong sense of insecurity.

There is also an element of extreme attraction in the above examples. Perhaps you know full well that other options exist. The other option just isn't as good, as sexy, as well-paying, or as interesting. In this case we are saying, "of all my options, I'd rather put up with abuse, plus get some of my needs met, than have neither." Here we have sacrificed our holistic well-being as a person for our well-being physically, financially, socially, etc.

"It's not their fault, they are just mentally ill."

In this case we are, again, making an excuse for this person. When we pin their behavior on something perceived to be outside their control, we are trying to take the blame away from them, too. Generally, the reason behind this is a mild form of fear. You don't think they will hurt you, or that you will be ostracized. But you fear *for* them. You want this person to be well, and you believe that if others see them for what they are, this person will be shunned. In this sense, extreme attraction is at also at play. We are blinded by the fear that, if people we trust *would hate* this person, then maybe they are a Bad Guy.

"I have to think of others before myself."

In this excuse we diminish ourselves. We are saying, "my needs matter less than those of my children, coworkers, or friends." Of course, this thinking is in error. If you are being abused, your kids will see that abuse and it will affect them. If you are being abused, your coworkers may also be at risk of the same treatment and should be warned. If you are being abused, your friends should be adults who can accept your choices and uphold you. The fear that we will be left unsupported during our time of greatest need is precisely what motivates this excuse. We are feeling insecure about our ability to care for and protect others.

Exercise:

Explore your own toxic relationships, or other toxic relationships you have seen. Consider what excuses were used when the abusive party caused harm. Consider what reasons a person had for maintaining the relationship. If the relationship ended, consider what reasons were given later on for its end.

Break down these excuses and try and see the true motivations behind them. Try and work out which of the three reasons were at play there. Consider what the person's options truly were, and why they might have avoided those options.

If you have never to your knowledge been in or witnessed an abusive relationship which lasted, try and break down the remaining sentences from the start of the chapter.

"They never hit me."

"It's the community aspect I'd miss."

"I don't want to hurt them."

"They offer me something amazing, something I can't find anywhere else."

"I take the good days with the bad."

Lesson 7: Developing a habit of self-love.

You might have noticed throughout this chapter that the reasons we have for staying in toxic relationships all have one thing in common: a lack of self-love, or self-respect.

When we love and respect ourselves, we rarely fall prey to insecurity, extreme attraction, or fear. Think of the most confident, self-loving person you know. If you aren't sure about real people, go back to a celebrity or fictional character who is known for being self-confident. Now look at the statements in the last exercise. Can you imagine this person saying any of that?

Of course not. But why not?

Because that person loves themselves and respects themselves. If their partner was psychologically abusive, they would not say, "They never hit me." They would say, "Bye!" If they felt that their partner connected them to other people, they would not fear the lack of community bonding. They would seek to sustain the community on their own, or to create or find a new community. This person will not allow themselves to be treated like trash by anyone, for anyone, or for anything.

That is the sort of mentality we need to cultivate. Not the complete "I don't care" attitude of these people. As we shall see later on, they may have their own issues, even if they aren't Bad Guys! We need to develop a self-love and self-respect so powerful that we will not allow ourselves to be treated poorly. We need to be as protective of ourselves as we are of our best friends, children, or pets. We need to see someone trying to take advantage of us and think, "How dare they! Not on my watch!"

Exercise:

Later on, in the last two chapters, we will explore other ways of giving ourselves a little love and respect, as well as how and why we should look after ourselves in general. To start off, consider yourself. Think about yourself not from the inside looking out, but from the outside looking in.

Who do you see? How would you describe this person? What do you think this person wants from life? Do they deserve it?

Imagine someone walked up to you today with all your same problems and asked you for help. Would you advise them to do what you are doing right now? Or to do something differently?

Being able to step back from our own identity and to consider ourselves, not from our ego or our inner critic, but as people like everyone else, can be very healing. It is important to practice this skill regularly, so that it becomes a habit. Too much introspection can make us judge ourselves harshly, much more so than we would judge anyone else. When we think of ourselves as a person, we are more likely to take our own advice, defend ourselves, and look after ourselves.

CHAPTER SIX: NARCISSISM AND THE DELUSION OF IMPORTANCE

Now we will begin to explore some of the signs and symptoms of the personalities which make up our Bad Guys. It is important to realize that Bad Guys are as diverse as the rest of us, and just as full of nuances. Not every Bad Guy has every sign and symptom, and none of the signs and symptoms are universal. But enough of these traits intertwined are sure to create a Bad Guy. So even if they look sweet and nice, are small, young and innocent, or do you favors, if you meet someone with many of these traits, run for the hills.

Studies have been conducted about the different mental state of Bad Guys for a long time, and the DSM, a medical text documenting mental health problems, has several definitions which explain Bad Guys. We will begin with one of them: Narcissism.

A narcissist sees themselves as special and more important than others. All the diagnostic criteria in the DSMV, as well as the other traits of narcissists that psychologists have suggested, focus on that one central personality flaw.

The DSMV lists the following requirements to diagnose a patient with Narcissistic Personality Disorder. **Please bear in mind that the full disorder and narcissistic leanings are different!** Someone can be narcissistic without being a full narcissist, and, in fact, many Bad Guys have four or five of these traits without having the full set. Here we will explore what each one means related to narcissism itself.

1. Has a grandiose sense of self-importance.

What does this mean?

It means that our narcissistic person really, really thinks they are much more important than others. They think of themselves the same way we think of our role models, parents, mentors, or idols.

What harm does it do?

When someone puts themselves on a pedestal, then we know they will never think of us as their equals. To them, they are royalty and the rest of the world resides underneath them. And we all know how badly Medieval royalty treated the peasants.

2. Is preoccupied with fantasies of unlimited success, power, brilliance, beauty, or ideal love.

What does this mean?

This means the narcissistic person basically lives in their own fantasies. We all have goals, of course, and we all daydream. At the end of the day, normal people know that our fantasies will never be real. We set more modest goals for ourselves, take pride in them, and enjoy them. The narcissist cannot do this. For them, a modest goal is a failure. They need to have a perfect relationship, a perfect career, a perfect identity, or they have failed.

What harm does it do?

When you live in your own fantasies, it's a bit like hallucinating. Everyone else knows the pink elephant isn't there, but the hallucinator does not. Likewise, the narcissist does not actually know that their unlimited greatness is just a fantasy! To them, it is a reality, either right now, or for the future. They will stop at nothing to attain it, in much the same way we will fight for our rights and victories. And yet unlimited greatness is too perfect to be true. Even when a narcissist reaches one of their goals, they are dissatisfied because it is still not perfect.[15]

3. Believes that he or she is "special" and unique and can only be understood by, or should associate with, other special or high-status people (or institutions).

What does this mean?

This means that they categorize people based on how important they believe them to be, and only want to associate with the most important people. The grain of truth here is that birds of a feather do flock together: we do tend to try and associate with people we believe are like us. The narcissistic person will try and associate only with people they believe are perfect, and hope for that perfection to rub off on them.

What harm does it do?

Because the narcissistic person will only associate with perfect people, everyone is at risk. People who are obviously imperfect from the start are thrown away like trash, but even the people the narcissist likes are at risk. Why? Because nobody is actually perfect, and as soon

---

15 Wallace, D. (2014) Narcissistic Rage and Addiction.

as the rose-tinted glasses come off the narcissist will be angry that you "tricked" them into thinking you were perfect.

4. Requires excessive admiration.

What does this mean?

The narcissistic person needs constant awe, respect, and praise, even for minor things. And they will continue to seek praise for things where they have already received praise.

What harm does it do?

Continually massaging someone's ego is not a relationship, but when you are living with a narcissistic person, that is what your relationship will consist of at the end of the day.

5. Has a sense of entitlement.

What does this mean?

We all have things we believe we deserve, either because they were promised to us, like our wages, or because we believe everyone ought to get them, like being treated with dignity. A narcissist steps outside of that normal social order and instead demands to be treated better or differently than others, even when this has not been agreed upon.

What harm does it do?

A narcissistic person will expect to be admired, to be rewarded, to always win contests and competitions, to get their perfect date, etc. But the narcissist can't always win. So, what happens when they lose? A combination of rage and denial. Rage because they feel they have been betrayed. And denial because they will suddenly decide they never wanted that thing, that the competition is rigged, or that the thing is different to how they imagined it. Anything is better than accepting their own failure. This leads to serious inconsistencies in how they behave, making them unreliable, dangerous people to be around.

6. Is interpersonally exploitative.

What does this mean?

This means that to a narcissistic person, other humans are just things. Either a means to an end, or an object to own and to use.

What harm does it do?

Quite obviously, if you reduce other people to objects, you will hurt them. We don't consider the feelings of a fork, or how a download will affect our computer beyond our ability to use it again. Likewise, a narcissist will only worry about the well-being of other humans as long as their well-being is also in the narcissist's best interests. And when it isn't? Then they won't get a second thought.

7. Lacks empathy: is unwilling to recognize or identify with the feelings and needs of others.

What does this mean?

Unlike antisocial or psychopathic people, whose empathy is literally missing, a narcissist often has stunted empathy. It's not that they can't see you are in pain, or relate to your trials, it's that they don't want to, because thinking about you would get in the way of thinking about themselves.

What harm does it do?

When someone forces themselves to push consideration and empathy out of their minds and focus on themselves alone, they fall back to hedonism and treating other people like tools again.

8. Is often envious of others or believes that others are envious of him or her.

What does this mean?

A narcissistic person is completely focused on social order. This means that they will always be comparing themselves to others, and assume others are also continually comparing themselves to the narcissist.

What harm does it do?

This constant comparison puts the narcissist's defenses up high. They are always afraid that someone else might try their same tricks on them and will often see any attempts to help them as manipulation. The nicer you are to a narcissist, the more paranoid you will make them.

9. Shows arrogant, haughty behaviors or attitudes.

What does this mean?

The narcissistic person is rude and inconsiderate. Again, like the rulers of Medieval Europe, the narcissist thinks they are above everyone else, and especially above the rules that apply to others.

What harm does it do?

Because the narcissist thinks they are better than you, they will act that way too. They will demand to see managers even when they are in the wrong, insist that they can do things to you which nobody can do to them, and generally bully other people.[16]

I am sure you can see now why it is that narcissistic behaviors can be so troublesome, even if the person does not have true Narcissistic Personality Disorder! Even one of these behaviors, on its own, can make a good relationship toxic. A few together and you have a Bad Guy, even when they are not a "true" narcissist!

This list is by no means complete. Many academics have spent a lifetime breaking down the nuances of narcissism, and the definitions and diagnoses are always changing and developing. However as of today, those are the main nine characteristics of narcissists.

Lesson 8: Spotting Narcissists.

Spotting a narcissist in the wild is harder than doing so in theory. On paper, the person who surrounds themselves with people quick to do their bidding, can't take a joke, and brags about their achievements is a narcissist, like the stereotypical high school jock. And the person who is shy, dismisses praise, and is friendly and forgiving is the opposite of a narcissistic. In reality, it's just not so clean cut.

Most of us already know that the popular kids at our high school were popular for a reason, and it was normally because they were *not* narcissists. They were probably gifted, but they were also kind, friendly, giving people. On the other hand, the kids we considered "creepy" were probably not just quiet, but antisocial and demanding. There may have been a few exceptions, but in general the stereotype that popular, successful, and proud people are narcissists and unpopular, unsuccessful, and shy people are not, is wrong.

And so is the more recent stereotype that it's the other way around. Some psychologists for

---
16 American Psychiatric Association. (2013). Diagnostic and statistical manual of mental disorders (5th ed.).

a very long time stuck with the idea that unpopular and awkward kids were more selfish and narcissistic, because they were compensating for their social flaws. Successful people, such as politicians, are also narcissists.[17]

The truth lies somewhere in the middle: Narcissists are often very gifted, skilled, or successful in one area, and it is this slight superiority that feeds their ego. But then they hold a lot of the rest of their lives to that same standard and it doesn't match up. A high school footballer or an artistic kid are great examples. If they accept that they are good at something but not at everything then they could be proud, but not narcissists. But if they are continually hung up on their perceived failings and demanding perfection of themselves in areas where they are not gifted, then they are at risk of developing narcissistic behaviors. It is for this reason that spotting a narcissist is hard: narcissism is an internal process, not something people wear on their sleeves.

However, there are some tells that are pretty obvious. Some recent research has found that most narcissists are aware that they are narcissists. Because in a narcissist's mind they are perfect, they embrace their own diagnosis. This means that many narcissists can be identified just by asking them, "Are you narcissistic/egoistic/selfish?" Most will answer honestly! [18]

That said, when a narcissist wants to manipulate us, this greater awareness of their own flaws is damaging to us. Unlike in the past where a narcissist had no clue who or what they were, now that they know they are narcissists they are getting better at hiding it. Which means we need to look more closely for the subtle signs of narcissism.

Exercise:

To detect narcissists in your life and work out whether someone you know exhibits the behaviors, you need to watch them when the going gets tough. We are all geared for survival and self-preservation in desperate situations. A narcissist is geared for self-preservation at

---

17 Freud, S. (1914) *Psychopathology of Everyday Life*; translated by A. A. Brill. PUBLISHED: New York: The Macmillan Company.

18 Linden S. and Rosenthal, S. A. (2015) Measuring narcissism with a single question? A replication and extension of the Single-Item Narcissism Scale (SINS). *Personality and Individual Differences. Vol 90. pp238-241.* Elsevier.

all times. Whether it is refusing to part with money they owe, blaming their mistakes on others, or lying to get a job or promotion, the narcissist always does whatever gets *them* ahead, no matter how it affects other people.[19]

Write down the last ten interactions you had with a person you think is narcissistic. Write out whether the outcome was positive or negative for you, positive or negative for them, and positive or negative for others. Now ask yourself if the positive outcomes for you and others were intentional... or just part of getting the narcissist what they wanted. If all ten interactions benefited them, often at the expense of others, you could be dealing with a narcissist.

---

[19] Whitbourne, S. K. (2012) Don't Be Fooled by a Narcissist. *Psychology Today.* PsychologyToday.com

CHAPTER SEVEN: MACHIAVELLIANISM IS NOT JUST PRAGMATISM

A lot of us, especially those of us who are a bit less emotional, like to think we are pragmatic. Even if you haven't heard the word "pragmatism" before, chances are you are familiar with the ideas behind it:

Pragmatism is the belief that a good solution, or the best possible solution, is the noblest goal for any thought or action.

In a pragmatic mindset, the universe is continually changing and evolving. Justice is not an end goal but something that's always one step away from us, and logic is a tool to help us reach true goodness and happiness.

For example, under pragmatism you might accept a job you don't want to give you time to work toward the one you do want Pragmatism means taking your experience of the world and accepting some compromises in order to reach the best possible end for all.

However, the Bad Guys like to corrupt things to suit themselves. Much the same way that they corrupted self-respect into narcissism, they corrupted pragmatism into Machiavellianism. Machiavellianism, if you have not heard the word before, can be summed up in one sentence:

The ends justify the means. [20]

Of course, there is a bit more to it than that. But that belief lies at the core of Machiavellian philosophy. It has one distinct difference from pragmatism. Under pragmatism we see the world holistically. For example, we take the job we do not want because we understand that in the short term we have less money, but in the long term we have *some* money and more

---

[20] Jain, K. and Bearden, J. N. (2011) Machiavellianism and Overconfidence. INSEAD.

time. A pragmatist would not accept a job that stopped them getting their ideal job completely, and they would not lie to get their ideal job instead.

Under Machiavellianism there is no big picture. There is just the end result. A Machiavellian person is more idealistic than pragmatic. To them, the ideal job is the *only good outcome*. So not only will they turn down the job they do not want, but they will lie and cheat and do anything it takes to get the ideal job, even if this means they are not ready for it.

Machiavellianism allows Bad Guys to convince us to do their bidding.

Deep down we all want to reach our goals eventually, and we all understand that other people want to reach their goals, too. Deep down we all want to be pragmatic about it. We want to make the decisions that hurt as few people as possible, help as many people as possible, and slowly but surely move us toward our end goal.

As we have seen, the line between "The noblest goal is chasing the best solution" and "The ends justify the means" is very, very fine. The main difference is that the pragmatic noble goal involves everyone's well-being, whereas the Machiavellian ends involve only the success of the ideal.

To push us into following their Machiavellian plans and not our own pragmatic ones, the Machiavellian person must, therefore, persuade us that their goal is also our goal and everyone else's goal.

This theory comes from Niccolo Machiavelli's book "The Prince". He explained the ways in which someone who wanted to be a ruler could manipulate society to convince people to side with their goals. There is a big debate about whether Machiavelli actually believed this was good or was just trying to avoid being killed by angry rulers, but one thing is undeniable: a Machiavellian approach to power works.

Most politicians rise to power and stay in power by convincing us that they are acting selflessly. When we vote for someone we are not thinking, "this person wants to be in power for status and money", we are usually thinking "this person has some good points about important topics and will look out for my best interests". Likewise, cult leaders and dictators avoid being overthrown, even though they are outnumbered, because the followers believe the leader is looking after them.

A Machiavellian person always tries to get money, power, and love from people, no matter what it costs. But because they need *you* to make sacrifices for *their goal*, they will try to convince you that their goal is your goal, too. [21]

Take for example an experience I had when an uncle of mine asked me for a loan. I had heard he did not pay back money he borrowed. So, I refused. Then he used the Machiavellian technique. He told me that if I gave him the loan, he would use it to get a better car, and I could use it. This was very appealing to me. I needed a better mode of transportation, but could not afford the car on my own. He promised it would be a nice car, he would repair it, and I just had to pay my share of fuel.

I'm sure you can guess what happened when I gave him the money. The car materialized, that much was true. But it was never available for me to use when I needed it. He always had priority. And on top of that he kept trying to get me to pay for half the fuel, even on months when I hadn't used it.

What he did was tell me what I wanted to hear. Otherwise known as lying. He told me there would be a car and that I could use it. Did I get my money's worth out of it? Of course not. My uncle's goal was to obtain a vehicle for himself without paying for it, no matter how it affected me. The lies were just part of the game.

Machiavellian people often act like this because Machiavellianism is characterized by an almost complete lack of morality. Bad Guys will stop at nothing as long as they get what they want in the end. They know we wouldn't just give them everything they ask for without believing there is something in it for us. So, they promise us money, new policies, a car, love,

---

[21] Machiavelli, N. (1532) *The Prince*.

or safety, if only we give them our ideas, vote, money, energy, or security first.

Lesson 9: Spotting Machiavellianism.

Machiavellianism in the wild can be hard to spot at times because the Machiavellian person is very good at convincing us they are pragmatic team players. Machiavellianism wouldn't be a problem if we could look at a politician and say, "they're just hungry for power", at a pyramid salesperson and say, "they just want our money", or at a romantic prospect and say, "they just want us for sex".

Like with narcissism, there are tell-tales of Machiavellianism which we can learn to spot. The biggest one is simple. The Bad Guy will ask you to make a sacrifice or take a risk. Taking risks isn't necessarily a bad thing, but we need to take risks we are comfortable with when we are ready for them. Making sacrifices willingly is not a bad thing either. But the Machiavellian pushes you to. Think about sales pitches if you want examples of Machiavellianism and forced risk or sacrifice:

Trial the product now, what have you got to lose?

If you don't vote for me, then you have no chance of a better water supply.

Together we can help reduce crime.

It only takes a few minutes of your day to make your neighborhood a better place.

For the same price as your nightly wine, you could buy our product.

These pitches are convincing, sure. That is why we see pitches like this everywhere because they work. What they are really doing is saying:
- We're a team!
- We're in it together!

- We will all benefit from the end result!
- The sacrifice is small!
- The risk is small!

They are trying to convince us to do something we haven't even thought about doing. If we were to swap the sales pitch for an admission of the true end goal, it becomes very obvious why they need us:

Trial the product now, what have you got to lose?

I need you to buy my product at least once to make back the ad money.

If you don't vote for me, then you have no chance of a better water supply.

I need you to vote for me, so I can get in power.

Together we can help reduce crime.

I need you to invest your time and energy in my scheme so that it becomes relevant.

It only takes a few minutes of your day to make your neighborhood a better place.

I need you to invest your time and energy into my scheme, so I don't have to use my time or energy.

For the same price as your nightly wine, you could buy our product.

I need you to sacrifice something you enjoy so you can afford my product.

They need *us*, but the sales pitch is designed to flip the message around and say we need them, or we need each other. Likewise, a Machiavellian individual will twist and turn their own interests to make it sound like it is in our interests:

It won't take long. Let's just go.

What is fifty bucks? It'll be fine. We can get it back later.

You don't really need to go out tonight. Stay and spend time with me.

Again, from time to time we will make sacrifices for friends, or friends will request a sacrifice. With a Machiavellian person there is no request. They will make it sound like it was our idea, in our best interests, and like they were just helping. [22]

Exercise:

Think about times people have recently asked you for help. If you can't think of recent ones, make a point of writing down the times when people ask you for help over the next week.

Ask yourself:

What did they ask for?

How did they phrase it?

Who benefits from the end result?

What do they get out of it?

Did they try and make it sound like a shared goal?

Did they push you into accepting a sacrifice or a risk without giving you time to think it over?

Did you feel used?

---
[22] Jain, K. and Bearden, J. N. (2011) Machiavellianism and Overconfidence. INSEAD.

You will be slightly surprised by how many Machiavellian interactions you have every day.

Fear not: not everyone who does this is a Machiavellian person, or a Bad Guy! We live in a world where we have been told that to get ahead, especially in work, we need to be Machiavellian. You may even catch yourself doing it from time to time.

Like with the narcissist, the key is consistency. Does this person ever ask for help politely? Do they ever help you out? Do they ever make the sort of sacrifice they are asking you to do? If the answer to those questions is 'yes', then they are just someone else trapped by social norms. But if the answer to all those questions is 'no', then you are dealing with someone Machiavellian.

CHAPTER EIGHT: IT'S ALL ABOUT ME – SOLIPSISM EXPLORED

Once again, like with pragmatism, solipsism is originally a perfectly valid philosophical theory. In fact, it is more of a thought experiment. Under solipsism we wonder whether we may be the only person in the world. An example of this theory is the brain in a jar thought experiment. If we are just a brain in a jar, and everything we see, think or feel is just electrical impulses, then is the world real, and do consequences matter?

The idea is that we cannot trust our experiences because they have all come from our brain, so they could all be dreams, hallucinations, or implanted by a machine. We have no true way of knowing if the people around us are real people, if they experience the same things we do, or if they are just simulations. The whole point is to make us reconsider what we know about other people and accept we do not live in their heads.

It is a fun exercise to play. It can even help us to understand people who are very different to us. And yet, at the end of the day, we all agree that even if we are a brain in a jar, it is better to play it safe and assume other people are humans with their own thoughts, feelings, and motivations. [23]

What happens when someone does this all the time? Solipsism can become pathological. And by pathological, I mean the person is not in control of their solipsism. They did not say, "Hey, this is a neat thought experiment." They just always act like they are the only person with logic, insight, and abstract thoughts. They treat other people like television characters, animals, or machines at all times.

It can be argued that solipsism is a sort of narcissism. The main difference is that narcissists are often aware they are narcissists. Even if they are not aware, when we tell them it makes sense to them. A narcissist can be so aware of their problem that they hide it and work around it. They learn to be, or at least act like, a better person. Not so with a solipsist. A solipsist is unable of thinking of other people as having brains.

---

[23] Speaks, J. (2007) Wittgenstein on the subject and solipsism. University of Notre Dame.

They think they can predict your behavior. They are angry with you when you do something differently to their prediction.

They think you will forget their misbehavior. They are angry and confused when you remember.

They think you know everything they know. They are confused when you have not read the same book or seen the same films.

They think you want the same things from life as they do. They are angry when you do not accept their gifts and confused when you are not jealous of their achievements.

They think you agree with them on all political and moral matters. They are confused when you disagree with them.

As such, solipsism is rarely connected to true mental disorders or personality disorders. In many ways, we could call solipsism "just being a bit of a dick". Because this behavior is really obvious most of the time we can just cut them out of our lives and move along. But when someone like this becomes a part of our lives it can be very difficult to live normally. When we go to school with them, work with them, or they are our parents, siblings, or children, we cannot just cut them off. In many ways, we would feel bad because we know they aren't doing it on purpose. They just don't understand that we are people, too. Intentionally or not, they will ruin our lives.

Take, for example, the ex-girlfriend of mine who used to steal my money for shopping sprees. Now, we could say she was being Machiavellian and just exploiting me. There is a problem with that it was nowhere near calculated enough to be Machiavellian. She was living with me at the time, which would make her stealing super obvious and make her vulnerable. She was always promising she would stop, but then would start and would make no extra effort to hide it. She was literally not aware of her own problem.

Which brings me back to solipsism. A solipsist does not realize they live in their own heads, because we need to step outside our own head to know there is more to the world. A bit like a baby in the womb has no way of knowing what the world is like, a solipsist has no way of knowing what other people are like. To them we are no different to characters on a screen. This is how they hurt us.

When was the last time you worried about whether your favorite TV character was doing alright? Have you ever wondered if your toaster minds being used for making breakfast? Of course not. We have some degrees of separation between people and everything else. Even when we do consider an animal to be equal to humans, we lift the animal, declaring it a "person", we do not lower humans to the level of animals.

For a solipsist all humans are animals, or objects! Just as we consider characters and objects just that, they never consider *you* other than for the influence you have in their lives. My ex-girlfriend wasn't using my money because she was being cold and calculating. She was using it because, in her mind, my purpose in life was to give her money. That was why she kept doing it even after moving in with me, and even after promising to stop. She could not understand that I am a human being with my own feelings, thoughts, and goals.

This is why we avoid people like this whenever we can, and why it is very dangerous when we are stuck in a relationship, even a casual relationship, with a solipsist. However, there are ways of identifying them and ways of managing them which can help us in our day to day lives. [24]

Lesson 10: Spotting the solipsist.

Solipsists are very easy to spot, and chances are you already know and dislike the solipsists in your life. They are overly concerned with themselves and will spend hours on what matters to them, but barely give minutes to anyone else. They expect the people around them to help them but will not return the favor. They seem to have empathy because seeing others suffer makes them sad... but when the suffering is gone they will forget about it, and sometimes

---

[24] Strawson, P.F. (1959) *Individuals, an essay in descriptive metaphysics.* Methuen.

they will even "solve" the problem by avoiding looking at or talking to those who are suffering. In short, they are entitlement made flesh.

However, we must distinguish them from three similar types of person: narcissists, autistic people, and people from a disconnected background.

We have already observed that the difference between solipsists and narcissists is that a narcissist knows that they are selfish and enjoys being selfish. Unlike the narcissist, the solipsist will condemn selfishness and maybe even do nice and selfless things when they feel very bad about themselves. They will never be kind out of anything but guilt or sadness, and they are unable to truly empathize with the people they are helping. They are just helping to make themselves feel good.

Many people who seem to treat others as objects are not selfish solipsists, but rather autistic. A huge characteristic of autism is an inability to relate socially. But this is different from an inability to empathize! Autistic people may treat you the way someone would treat an object, but it is not out of malice. Rather, they just do not know how to treat you and revert back to a "neutral" behavior.

Unlike the solipsist, the autistic person wants you to be happy, and is not wholly selfish. If you tell them and show them how you want to be treated they will often adapt. On the other hand, the solipsist, at the suggestion that they are acting in a way that hurts you, will get angry and confused, and refuse to change. They will blame you for making them feel bad, and not themselves for treating you poorly.

Finally, some people who seem not to understand that other people are different from them may simply have had a sheltered life, or just a very different life to ours. There is nothing at all wrong or different about these people medically speaking. They just have no idea that, for example, some people have gone without food for days or weeks. They do not understand that some people work so much that they cannot sleep right or can't afford medical care. These people are getting very rare thanks to how well information spreads, but they still exist. They learn very fast and are basically normal people once you get to know them.[25]

Exercise:

For this exercise I need you to look back on the "weird, annoying, selfish" people you have known. Compare them to the narcissist, the autistic person, the disconnected person, and the solipsist. Which one do they most resemble? What makes you say that?

Lesson 11: Avoiding and handling the solipsist.

As we have already discussed, the biggest issue isn't spotting a solipsist. We can already tell that these people are trouble. We could tell before we knew what to call them, since we just used to call them "jerks". Now that we recognize their negative traits, sometimes we just cannot avoid their company. Either they are a relative, or they are someone we have to work with or study with.

So, what do we do when they are part of our lives? The first and most important strategy is simply to avoid them. We may feel guilty for doing this, because it will genuinely make them sad. We need to remember that it makes them sad the same way a remote control not working makes them sad. They are not experiencing the genuine loss of a friendship because you were never a friend to them, just a tool.

If you cannot avoid them, then you need to work out how to handle their behavior. The first step to handling a solipsist is to put yourself first. Seriously. The solipsist lives in their own head and is literally only thinking about themselves, so you can't treat the relationship as one of equals. If you want even a chance of surviving this, you need to put yourself first and give yourself a fair chance. Whatever they do, ask, say, or suggest, make a point of asking yourself if that helps you at all.

You also need to remain polite and keep emotions low. Unlike a narcissist or a Machiavellian, a solipsist has very intense emotions, much like a toddler. The solipsist cannot handle it when you are hurt because it makes them feel bad. They also cannot handle being refused,

---
25 Locke, J. (1959) *Essay Concerning Human Understanding.* Dover.

corrected, interrupted, directed, or anything else which stops them from being the center of their own universe. So how do you handle a person who acts like a toddler? You treat them like a toddler. [26]

Use short and simple sentences. Do not say things that are ambiguous or make small talk. If they start talking about themselves, acknowledge them with positive words and then change the topic back to the subject you need to discuss. Remember that it is pointless to argue with solipsists, as they will just get angry and not change their behavior You just have to gently direct them toward the solution that ends the interaction as soon as possible.

Exercise:

If you currently have a relative or a coworker who is a solipsist, I want you to make a point of passing by their location at some point in the near future.

When you are around them, make sure that you keep the interaction positive and relaxed. Do not take anything they say or do to heart. Remember: they are a toddler. Your mission is to get what you came for and leave.

---

[26] Ruesch, J. (1948) The Infantile Personality. University of California Medical School.

CHAPTER NINE: ANTISOCIAL PERSONALITIES AND SOCIAL ORDER

Antisocial personality disorder is the official psychiatric term for what the rest of us call a psychopath. We often talk about psychopathy like it is some sort of a "serial killer mental illness" which will make a person go around committing serious crimes, but the reality is not that simple.

Psychopathy is defined by a complete lack of empathy and too much impulsivity. This doesn't mean they are ready to go out and hurt people any more than you go out of your way to kick rocks. But it does mean that to them you are nothing more than a rock, and that if hurting you crosses their mind, it could happen. Which actually makes a real psychopath more dangerous than a stereotypical movie psychopath.

The DSMV says that psychopaths have certain behaviors. However, it is again important to remember that any of these behaviors can be dangerous and that a person who does any of these things regularly is a risk, even if they are not a true psychopath!

1. Failure to conform to social norms with respect to lawful behaviors as indicated by repeatedly performing acts that are grounds for arrest.

What does this mean?

The important part to note here is "failure to conform to social norms". A strong emphasis is placed on legal versus illegal behavior because obviously this impacts society the most, and in our culturally varied world, what is a social norm for one person may be a strange custom for another. The key thing to remember is that a psychopath does not follow the rules. Whether it's the law, social expectations, office rules, or civilized behavior, they do not conform. They live and act only for themselves.

What harm does it do?

When someone does not care about any rules or norms at all, they will break them if they want to. This means a psychopath is more likely than a normal person to do something illegal, dangerous, or unpleasant.

2. Deceitfulness, as indicated by repeated lying, use of aliases, or conning others for personal profit or pleasure

What does this mean?

Quite simply: they do not care about the truth. The truth is a social norm that almost every society values, but because it is a norm, it doesn't matter to the psychopath.

What harm does it do?

As we have already discussed, telling the truth ourselves and being able to tell when someone is lying are important cornerstones of socializing. With a psychopath you are always in the dark.

3. Impulsivity or failure to plan ahead

What does this mean?

This trait is not related to their lack of empathy. It is actually the other key trait of a psychopath. It may not be obvious, but they are continually in what we call fight or flight mode, always running on adrenaline. This can be confusing because often they look like they are planning everything so carefully. In reality? That calm, collected face and that "I planned this all along!" speech are lies. Because they are used to adrenaline, they may be able to hide their energy, but they are always looking for their next rush.

What harm does it do?

When we enter fight or flight mode it is usually for survival reasons. An animal attacking us, a loud sound in the middle of the night, or a fight are good examples. Our body then tells us to run or to fight, and we do it without thinking. This is a good response because thinking would waste valuable time where we could be in danger. Now imagine if every decision was split-second, you followed through on almost everything you considered doing, and you had to second-guess everything decision because you acted rashly. Chances are you would do a lot of risky things.

Many psychopaths adapt as they grow up, and eventually learn to pause and force themselves to think instead of act on impulse. But even the best-trained psychopath slips up, so they will eventually do something dangerous on an impulse.

4. Irritability and aggressiveness, as indicated by repeated physical fights or assaults

What does this mean?

Again, this is because of their increased stress response. All it takes is a slightly tense situation and they break into aggression like they were being attacked by a bear.

What harm does it do?

Obviously, someone being ready for a fight as soon as you bump into them is not a good thing for society.

5. Reckless disregard for safety of self or others

What does this mean?

Again, fight or flight is to blame. In a dangerous situation we rarely have time to calculate the least dangerous option. Instead, we just focus on getting rid of the threat.

What harm does it do?

Because the psychopath is acting completely on impulse, they will not be able to stop and consider everyone's safety. They may not even care. This, in day to day life, is definitely not a good thing.

6. Consistent irresponsibility, as indicated by repeated failure to sustain consistent work behavior or honor financial obligations

What does this mean?

Again, when you are an impulsive person you do not think about long-term things. Psychopaths are unable to consider how they need to act for the next day, let alone weeks, months, or years. Some *psychopathic* people are able to act like psychopaths and still plan ahead, but a true psychopath, under the DSMV definition, would not be able to do so.

What harm does it do?

Because they treat people like they will never need them, spend like money will never be scarce, and treat work like it will be there forever, they are completely unprepared for when these things disappear. This not only affects them, but everyone around them.

7. Lack of remorse, as indicated by being indifferent to or rationalizing

What does this mean?

Going back to their lack of empathy, a psychopath does not feel bad about the results of their actions. Someone could do all the above and although they would be a dangerous person, they would not be a psychopath. Psychopaths are genuinely comfortable being who they are. They do not mind hurting people. Much like the solipsist, the only time they regret their actions is when they are suffering the consequences. And even then, when the consequences end, they rarely learn from their mistake. They often do the same things repeatedly.

What harm does it do?

This means that everything a psychopath does to hurt you will happen repeatedly. You can never correct them. No matter what you say or do, as soon as they are free, they will repeat their behavior and cause the same damage again. [27]

At this point, you are probably starting to see why psychopathy was renamed Antisocial Personality Disorder. It is literally a threat to society. Civilization was built by people looking forward, putting aside their primitive animal instincts, and looking out for one another, to build a better future for all. Psychopathy is literally the opposite of civilization and, in that sense, the opposite of humanity. Everything that makes us different from animals is missing in a psychopath. They are the raw, primitive human beast that we all wish had been left behind.

It is important to remember this, because it helps us to understand psychopaths. On some level, a psychopath lives within all of us. They do not have anything extra that we are missing, but we have extra traits that make us more civilized. We have the ability to control our instincts. We have forward planning. We have empathy, even for people we have never met. They lack all of this. They are us, without our ability to think about the future or to care for others. [28]

---

[27] American Psychiatric Association. (2013). Diagnostic and statistical manual of mental disorders (5th ed.).

[28] Yang et al (2005). Volume Reduction in Prefrontal Gray Matter in Unsuccessful Criminal Psychopaths. BIOL PSYCHIATRY 2005;57:1103-1108 University of Southern California.

It is also important to consider that not all psychopaths are dangerous to us. All psychopaths could potentially harm us, but many of them go about their lives without ever hurting anyone or doing anything obvious. They are acting on impulse every day of their lives, but not everyone has criminal impulses. We hear a lot about the psychopaths who have an impulse to kill, have constant sex, or binge eat, because the media loves sensational stories. But 1-2% of humans are psychopaths, and most of them are just normal, everyday people on the outside.[29]

That makes them more dangerous, because out of every 100 people you meet, one or two of them are the sort of person who, if they really felt like it, would hurt you without a second thought.

Lesson 12: Spotting the psychopath.

The DSMV diagnostic criteria for Antisocial Personality Disorder is a great place to start when we are trying to spot psychopaths, or people with psychopathic tendencies. A psychopath acts on impulse, which makes them fairly easy to spot.

Psychopaths are usually unsuccessful people. We often think of psychopaths as being incredibly successful in their chosen field, whether it's the ruthless billionaire CEO, or the serial killer with hundreds of bodies in the basement. Really, psychopaths are more likely to be working at a fast food chain, or people arrested for starting scuffles in bars. Being successful takes self-control and lots of planning, two things most psychopaths lack.

If you do know a successful psychopath, chances are they succeeded thanks to luck. Lottery winners, people in the right place at the right time, or people with a unique talent can make up for their lack of planning ability. Another way psychopaths succeed is by exploiting the hard work of others. Many wealthy psychopaths had wealthy parents or married very wealthy people. Most psychopaths who climbed their own way to the top did this by letting other people do the work and taking the credit for themselves. This is as close as a

---

[29] Reiko, G. (2016) Differentiating Successful Psychopaths from Non-psychopathic Controls. Texas State University.

psychopath can get to forward planning and is very rare.

Psychopaths will be hedonists. This doesn't automatically mean a psychopath will be an overweight, alcoholic, shopaholic, nymphomaniac, because not everyone likes food, alcohol, consumables, or sex all that much. What it does mean is that everything a psychopath does is for their own pleasure. They will probably have a hard time staying in shape, have tried drugs at some point, and have a long list of past sexual partners. They could also be workaholics, or compulsive exercisers, if they genuinely enjoy these things. The key is that they avoid sacrifice like the plague and live just for pleasure.

Because they did not earn their successes, and because they are hedonists, psychopaths have a hard time holding onto wealth of any kind. A psychopath is more likely to be broke than other people with their income, less likely to own a house than other people of their age and with their income, and less likely to have anything else that comes with wealth, such as marriage, family, or status. Even if you know a successful psychopath, if you see them in a year's time they could be unsuccessful again.

Exercise:

When trying to work out if you know any psychopaths closely, look for unsuccessful people who are completely focused on their own pleasure. Usually, an unsuccessful person is focused on improving themselves, so they can succeed. A psychopath cannot learn, so they will happily stay unsuccessful as long as they can indulge their hedonistic lifestyle. They will only do the bare minimum to keep this lifestyle.

It is important to identify these people because they are exactly the ones who do dangerous things "out of nowhere". Do not be deceived if they are charismatic, funny, and sexually attractive. Psychopaths are often all these things, because looking like a nice person is the easiest way of manipulating people. It is important to not develop an intimate relationship with psychopaths, because they can suddenly turn against you. It is also important not to be cruel to them, or even to put too much trust in them. There is always the chance that they will decide you need to be hurt. Why? Just because they feel like it.

Do you know any psychopaths, or people with psychopathic tendencies? If you know someone you are not sure of, it is better to be careful. Assume they are psychopathic until they prove otherwise more than once. Your safety might depend on it.

CHAPTER TEN: SHALLOW AFFECT AND EMOTIONAL INTELLIGENCE

Shallow affect is a key aspect of many Bad Guy personalities and mental disorders. Narcissists, psychopaths, and borderlines, for example, all show shallow affect. When someone does not experience the same range or depth of emotions as the average person it's referred to as shallow affect.

To understand this, let's use the example of color. We all see color in some way unless we are blind. Some people may see colors more vividly, some people may see more differences between similar colors, but in general our experience of color is very similar. That is why most people enjoy combining similar colors. That is why we often agree on what paintings are fine art and which ones are not.

But then there are a few people who are color-blind. Some of these people do not see all the colors we see. For example, red and green may seem the same to them. Or red and brown. Or blue and yellow. They are simply missing some colors the rest of us take for granted.

Other color-blind people see all the same colors, but they are faded. They could separate red and green on a page, but they could not tell apart a richly colored item or something painted in pastels or dusky colors

People who are color-blind do not seriously suffer because of their condition. They have often lived with it their whole lives, and even if they have not, we adapt fast to changes in the way we see things. They just understand the world very differently to those who recognize color well. They may not react the right way in front of a stop sign. They may not be able to read a certain advertisement. They may not feel the same way we do about fashion or art.

If you swap color for feelings, then we have a perfect picture of shallow affect. Quite simply there are people out there who are missing feelings, or who do not experience any intensity in their feelings, or both. Maybe they cannot feel angry, disappointed, bored, irritated, or frustrated, only sad. Maybe they can feel all these things, but their feelings are never enough to get them to act. They have been a little bit annoyed, but never angry enough to shout or get physical. They have been sad, but never miserable enough to cry. The sort of extreme emotions that we see in films aren't just rare for these people: they are impossible, and probably very confusing.

Shallow affect does not have to be a bad thing for the sufferer or the people around them. You can go through your whole life without feeling the same feelings as other people and have no problems. To put this in perspective: there are feelings that many of us do not experience.

Schizophrenic, transsexual, and bipolar people often experience something called dissociation. They feel their body and their self is separate. Autistic people can experience a sensation of overwhelm caused by something meaningless to the rest of us. Schadenfreude, or epicaricacy, is the feeling of enjoying seeing someone else suffer. These are real feelings that some people experience, but that most of us will never really understand.

We are not incomplete for not having these feelings. We do not need these feelings to treat the people who have them as people. We can empathize with, relate to, and interact with these people despite not having the same feelings they have. It's about humanity, not shared experience. In much the same way, someone who has never been truly angry can empathize with, relate to, and interact with us. Even if they do not have our same experiences. Because there is one experience we all share: the experience of being human.

When we combine shallow affect and other Bad Guy symptoms, we get problems. This happens because some of the things which help us to be good people are based in emotion. Not everyone has a robust moral compass. Many, many people do not see the difference between "good" and "good for me", or "evil" and "bad for me". The way that these people know how to behave is by checking in with their feelings. Our emotions guide us and show us whether what we are doing is good or bad. This supports us morally and makes sure we make the right decisions for our civilization.

Guilt is an emotion nobody likes feeling, but a very important one. Guilt lets us know that society actively disapproves of something we've done. It makes us feel uncomfortable, even if nobody else knows about it. It encourages us not to do this again.

Without guilt, many people would be able to do the same bad things repeatedly because sometimes it can be hard to relate to the struggles and suffering of another person. But we can relate to their pain, sadness, or anger. So, we do, and then we experience guilt. When we cannot experience guilt, we cannot correct our behavior

Joy is an emotion that encourages us to keep doing the same things. This is why we experience joy when we eat great food, spend time with people we love, or do something kind.

Without joy, many people turn to simple rushes like sugar, drugs, sex, or games to make themselves feel good. There is no true accomplishment in these things, but they trigger our simplest reward instincts. This means we will do simple, instinctive things repeatedly, rather than deeper, more meaningful things that will make us happy in the long-term.

Shame is an emotion that lets us know how to fit in. Humans are social animals and we deeply want to fit in with a small, closely connected group. We experience shame when we break the rules or expectations of the group. The other side of shame is discomfort. We get uncomfortable when someone else does something that would make us feel ashamed.

Without shame, we do things that at best make our group feel uncomfortable, and at worst actively hurt it. Shame is our way of drawing boundaries that are not described by morals or by laws.

Anger is an emotion that lets us know when we have been hurt. Anger provides the courage we need to fight for the things we are passionate about. Sometimes when we get angry, we can effectively defend ourselves and our loved ones.

Without anger, we are at risk of getting hurt or abused. We could also allow our loved ones to be hurt and abused. Someone who does not experience anger may not care when they are wronged.

Fear is another emotion that lets us know when we have been hurt. Fear is present when there is something dangerous that we are not able to fight. When we get scared we are preparing to confront or avoid a threat.

Without fear, we risk running head-first into danger. We are also likely to get our loved ones involved in dangerous situations. As both fear and fearlessness feed off the emotions of others, our loved ones will not feel as scared because we seem fearless.

These are not the only emotions which could be missing in someone with shallow affect, but they are some of the most dangerous ones. Without even one of these emotions we could act in a way that hurts us or the people around us. Again, normally a person without these emotions will adapt. If they are also narcissistic, or solipsistic, then they may not notice or care that their lack of emotions hurts others.

Likewise, when emotions are numbed in general people can become dangerous and unpredictable. This happens in part because this person does not relate to us at all. And in part because humans like feeling things. Feelings are an integral part of our humanity. When someone does not have intensity in their feelings, then they will try and enhance their lukewarm response somehow.

Thrill-seeking is one way of enhancing feelings. Thrill-seekers will do anything to cause pain (e.g. martial arts) or fear (e.g. parachute jumping). They do these things because pain and fear trigger the release of feel-good hormones that will lift their mood a bit.

Over indulgence is another way of enhancing feelings. Over indulgers will keep doing the same thing repeatedly and compulsively to enjoy the positive feelings that come with fulfilling their simple instinctive needs.

Some people with shallow affect try and live feelings vicariously through others. Vicarious feelers will do nearly anything to get a reaction out of someone. It doesn't matter if the emotion is positive or negative, but the more intense the better.

All three of these ways of enhancing emotions are technically harmless and can be done safely. But when combined with literally any other Bad Guy behaviors they become a problem, and the more Bad Guy behaviors there are, the more dangerous the person could be. [30]

Lesson 13: Identifying shallow affect.

Identifying shallow affect may sound like a challenge, but it is actually really easy most of the time because our emotions are very visible on our faces and bodies. Most of the time we can tell when someone has normal emotions and when someone has shallow affect just by looking at them.

A person with normal emotions will show their emotions in the ways our culture deems acceptable. They will smile when something good happens. They will seem upset when something bad happens. How extreme their expressions are will vary. It depends on both our culture and on how outgoing the person is. But they will show their emotions whether they intend to or not.

Likewise, someone with shallow affect will not show much emotion, whether they intend to or not. They will seem a little stone-faced at all times and may not react to things that happen to them, whether they are good or bad. They might try and imitate normal expressions, but it will always seem insincere.

We can make mistakes when using this method. Most of these mistakes will be false positives, that is, we will assume someone has shallow affect when they do not. For example, someone from a more modest culture, or from a subculture like emo culture, may intentionally hide emotions. This could at first look like someone without much emotion. However, over time you will begin to see their own personal ways of showing their feelings.

---

[30] Cataldi, S.L. (1993) *Emotion, Depth, and Flesh: A Study of Sensitive Space: Reflections on Merleau-Ponty's Philosophy of Embodiment.* SUNY Press.

Sometimes we can get a false negative, which is when we assume someone has more depth of emotion than they do. This is rare but usually happens when someone with shallow affect knows they have shallow affect. The key to discovering these people is to catch them off guard. When surprised, it can take them a few minutes to work out what the "right" emotion is. If this person is cold and calm in unexpected situations, then they may have shallow affect.

Exercise:

A great exercise to help us identify shallow affect is identifying normal, healthy emotion levels. Spend some time looking at yourself in the mirror. When talking to friends and family, watch their eyes, eyebrows, mouth, and cheeks. You will slowly begin to notice what a normal emotional reaction looks like. There is a huge range of what is normal, of course! The more people you watch and the more varied situations you are in, the more you will discover the pattern of what is normal. And when you know what normal looks like, it is much easier to identify abnormal emotional reactions, for example shallow affect.

Again, always remember that shallow affect, on its own, is not always bad. But if you meet someone with shallow affect who is also, for example, selfish, or a liar, then you might be looking at a Bad Guy.

CHAPTER ELEVEN: "EVIL" - SADISM AND SCHADENFREUDE

Humans have this fixation on the concept of "evil". We are obsessed with it. Most world religion condemns it. Most human society tries to avoid it. Most people who act in a way that offends us earns the evil label. We try and base our lives around its existence, and around avoiding being anything like it.

However, "evil" does not exist anywhere in nature. No animal concerns itself with whether killing its food or its enemy is ethical. No animal worries whether its power comes from righteous means. They do not care if they are being good or being evil. It is an exclusively human concept.

So, what do we humans mean by this word? Often, we are quick to label an action "evil" when it comes from a strange human, which we would not consider evil if it came from a known person, or an animal. When someone we know does an "evil" thing we look for a motivation, for something to excuse them, to make sure they did not intend to cause harm.

If they hit a dog, but the dog was attacking their child, that is fine. If they stole food from a store because they were starving, that is fine. If they threw a stone through a window for no reason at all, we start considering them "bad" or "wicked", and if someone repeatedly does harmful things without cause, then they are "evil". Indeed, even if they are generally good people, if they do a particularly heinous thing for no reason, such as murder, they are automatically evil at the first offense.

In short: what we consider "evil" is harm for the sake of harm itself. It is impossible to go through life without causing any harm at all, so we all strive to cause the least harm possible. We justify harm when there is no other way. When someone causes harm for no reason, or causes harm when there was a better way, we consider them to be evil.

We also base our definition of "evil" on our own personal ethics. This happens because although we generally agree on what we consider harmful, we all place the severity on a different scale. For example, to an informed vegan, the lives of thousands of animals are more valuable than the quality of life of one human. To an informed omnivore, the quality of life of a human is more valuable than the lives of thousands of animals. If someone risked a human life to save an animal, the vegan would consider them good, but the omnivore would consider them bad, if not evil.

Very few people actually set out to cause harm for no reason! This is why it is easy to call strangers evil, but not friends. When someone is a stranger, we rarely know their motivation. When they are a friend, we can see that they were doing their best.

Nevertheless, there are some people who do set out to cause harm just because they want to hurt others. Even if you could ask them directly, their honest answer would be "I wanted to hurt someone." This desire to hurt others for no other reason than to see them squirm can be loosely divided into the sexually motivated desire and the socially motivated desire.

Sadism is the name we give to the behavior of someone who likes seeing others in pain because it brings them sexual pleasure. Although the term is used often, there are actually not many true sadists in the world. Most people are not sexually aroused by pain, no matter how much they strive to cause it. In fact, most people are actively turned off by seeing others suffer.

That said, sadism is based on natural behavior. On some level, pain and pleasure are deeply connected. Love bites, scratching, and other acts of primal lovemaking are things we would not tolerate outside of sex. We would consider it abusive if a partner choked and bit their lover as they did the laundry.

Some adventurous people make an exception in the bedroom to indulge their primitive urges to bite and scratch and bruise. Not only that, but the hormones released during sex make these things feel pleasant, rather than painful. Sadism is just a more extreme form of this natural urge.

A healthy sadist is someone who can compartmentalize their sadistic urges and only act them out with a willing, masochistic partner. They make special time for sex, find someone who enjoys the feeling of pain, and indulge in private, safely, without intent to cause lasting damage.

A toxic sadist is someone who is unable or unwilling to consider the well-being of others at all. They will not seek out a willing partner for private acts. Rather, they may be abusive in public, attack unwilling people, and cause real, lasting harm for the sake of their own sexual thrill. This sort of sadism is actually very rare. Most people who enjoy pain either engage in healthy sadism, or in schadenfreude.

Schadenfreude, or epicaricacy, is a term used to describe when someone simply finds the pain of others to be amusing.

We all experience this urge on some level. It usually manifests as either good-natured or vindictive. Sometimes we see a friend hurt themselves, or do something that cannot possibly end well, and so long as they are not badly hurt, their suffering amuses us. Sometimes we see someone do something we consider to be bad, or evil, and the consequences affect them in such a way we find it entertaining.

A healthy way of living out schadenfreude is when we simply enjoy the "karma" that others have earned, without doing them harm, and preferably helping them at the end. There is nothing evil about laughing when someone falls into the pool after trying to push you in. There is nothing wrong with feeling satisfaction when someone hurting a dog gets hit back. So long as we are not actively harming others for no reason, a little bit of schadenfreude is healthy and natural.

A toxic form of schadenfreude is when someone will actively hurt others for their own amusement. This usually manifests as bullying, though it can be more serious. The person who pushes others into the pool, insults their appearance, or tries to make them do things against their will is probably experiencing schadenfreude.

Whether it is sadistic or just for fun, taking pleasure in the suffering of others is a key component to many Bad Guys' behavior. Of course, some Bad Guys just don't care. But the ones who enjoy seeing you suffer are even more dangerous. A Bad Guy who does not care will at least stop causing suffering when they have what they want. A Bad Guy who enjoys your pain will keep on hurting you no matter how much they get.

For example, my girlfriend could have just enjoyed the easy life living with me provided for her. She did not. She seemed to enjoy seeing me squirm, so her bad behavior escalated to bullying. By the end, her desire to hurt me could no longer be ignored. Had she not bullied me, I might have justified her behavior for much longer and continued living with her.

Masochism naturally plays an enormous part in how this aspect of a Bad Guy unravels. Many victims of abuse find that they gain a feeling of power when they indulge in masochistic behavior. Again, healthy masochism exists. This is where the person enjoys pain and engages in it in a consensual, safe, controlled environment. They have a safe word, and outside of the bedroom the sadist is a normal, loving partner to them.

On the other hand, some masochists end up in relationships where they have no control and no safety at all. This is far more dangerous for them and invites Bad Guys to stay. On a more basic level, some victims of Bad Guys feel a sort of martyr complex. We shall explore this more in Chapter Fifteen.

At the end of the day, it is important to know where to draw the line. Even the most physically painful acts of sadism and masochism can be safe and healthy if done in a consenting, loving, compartmentalized environment. Even the gentlest, most casual of cruelties can be toxic and deeply scarring if done in a toxic and dangerous environment.

Lesson 14: Spotting sadism and schadenfreude.

Because, as mentioned, some types of schadenfreude are ridiculously common, it can be difficult to spot Bad Guys who enjoy acts of sadism and schadenfreude. It is very easy to justify someone's behavior, and most people, even Bad Guys, will offer an excuse to cover their less than pleasant acts.

"I was not feeling well."

"I didn't realize what I was doing."

"They hurt me first."

There is *always* an excuse. Always. What you need to do is separate the justifiable reasons from the excuses, to unmask evil.

Exercise:

A simple way of learning to detect sadism and schadenfreude is playing Devil's Advocate. First of all, look for someone undeniably evil. Then, see if you can justify their behavior somehow. This will show you how easy it can be to cover for a Bad Guy!

On the other hand, you have to consider scale. We label some people evil because they did not have to deliberately cause the harm. Even when they give us an excuse, we know there was a better way of solving their problem.

Therefore, when we are faced with someone who has done something we find to be atrocious, we need to step back a moment and analyze the situation before acting. Firstly, we need to ask ourselves if they had other options. And secondly, we need to ask ourselves if we are making excuses for them if we are playing Devils' Advocate. People should not be judged and labeled as evil without certainty of their underlying motivations.

Lesson 15: Separating the kinky from the dangerous.

Again, many people engage in sadomasochistic sexual behavior in a safe and healthy way. There is nothing wrong with any kink, however odd it may seem to others, as long as it is:

- Safe
- Empathetic
- Consensual

However, if you are practicing sadomasochistic sex, it is important to make sure that you are doing so in a safe, empathetic, and consensual way. It can be easy for a Bad Guy to blur the lines. They may insist, "you like this", "we agreed to this last time", or "I thought you wanted it" to cover up their abusive behavior.

It is therefore vital to set clear boundaries at all times, and to enforce them. And if your partner keeps trying to push, break, or bend your boundaries without your consent, then you know you are dealing with someone who is a Bad Guy.

Exercise:

Whenever you find yourself feeling uncomfortable about the level of sadism in your relationship, ask yourself the following questions:

1. Is this something new, which we need to discuss?
2. Have they asked for my permission to do this?
3. If I ask them to stop, do they stop?
4. Are they giving me time to adapt and feel good?
5. Are they limiting this to the bedroom and other sexual contexts?
6. Are they loving, caring, and affectionate in their own way after the act is complete?

If the answer to all those questions is a solid "yes", then you are in a healthy relationship full of safe, empathetic, consensual interactions. If the answer to any of those questions is "maybe" or "no", then you are in a relationship which may be dangerous or may just need more communication. But if the answer to half or more of those questions is "no", then you are dealing with a Bad Guy who is willing to put your safety behind their enjoyment.

CHAPTER TWELVE: SPOTTING A PATHOLOGICAL LIAR

Lying is a part of being a human. We all lie from time to time. Whether we consider lying right or wrong, it is important to note that it is normal, and that lying, in and of itself, does not make a person a Bad Guy.

If someone lies because they want to spare your feelings, because they are scared of an overblown reaction, or because they are ashamed, then they are probably just normal people. Likewise, if they lie once or twice a week, that is perfectly ordinary.

Pathological lying is different. Pathological liars lie compulsively. It is a matter of habit for them, which they often cannot stop even when they do not want to. Usually it has no clear end goal and can be so completely directionless that it can even hurt the liar themselves. They may stick to their guns and create elaborate fake worlds and backgrounds that they insist are real. Or they may lie at random, about whatever they feel like lying about at the time, often contradicting themselves. They just can't stop lying. [31]

It has actually been found that a pathological liar's brain is wired differently to a normal person's brain. Whereas a normal person, when asked a question or given a turn in a conversation, will start thinking and formulating a response based on the truth, a pathological liar will not. They will begin lying before they have even had time to think of a reply. Not only that, but when telling the truth, a part of their brain lights up showing discomfort. They are literally hardwired to lie to us. [32]

There is no set way of catching a pathological liar. Even the APA refuses to include it in the DSM, because the tells are so variable from person to person. Psychiatrists maintain it is hard to tell when a pathological liar is to blame for their actions and when they are not. It is a very hard thing to define and detect, even for trained professionals.

---

[31] Dike, C.C., Baranoski, M., and Griffith, E.E. (2005) Pseudologia Lying Revisited. *The Journal of the American Academy of Psychiatry and the Law.* 33 342-349.

[32] Biever, C. (2005) Liars' brains make fibbing come naturally. *New Scientist. Reprint from British Journal of Psychiatry, Oct 2005.*

Pathological lying is more a symptom of many different psychological and behavioral disorders. Very few people are pathological liars without suffering from a disorder. And even those who do not suffer a disorder will also display other behaviors, like narcissism or sadism, which are a more important part of their problem than lying. Quite simply, pathological lying is a sign of a problem. Or a way a problem manifests. It is not a condition in and of itself.[33]

Sometimes a pathological liar will weave their lies together to make themselves look better. This is quite rare, as usually this sort of lying is controlled, and therefore not pathological. However, some cases have been identified where an individual commits so much to a lie that they continue to lie pathologically to defend it.

Sometimes a pathological liar will genuinely believe their lies. This is also rare but happens in cases such as when someone is a narcissist, or when they suffer from other delusional ideas about themselves. They create an ideal world where they are everything they want to be. It is very difficult to persuade them that their lies are not real.

In most cases, a pathological liar lacks direction. They know they are not telling the truth. They contradict or even harm themselves. They just cannot stop. Even when it's not being done for any particular reason, pathological lying can harm relationships. At the very least it will make them a difficult person to live with. If someone will say they are outside waiting for you when they are not, or that they made food when they have not, you cannot rely on them at all. You always have to check and second-guess everything they say or do which can be utterly exhausting.[34]

Pathological liars, like any liar, do not just lie with their words, they also lie by omission. This is when they simply do not tell you something. Of course, we cannot always expect the other people in our lives to tell us all about everything they have said, done, or thought that day. But when someone consistently forgets to tell you things, especially things which

---

[33] Hausman, K. (2003) Does Pathological Lying Warrant Inclusion in DSM? *Clinical & Research News.* Psychnews.psychiatryonline.org

[34] Dike, C.C. (2008) Pathological Lying: Symptom or Disease? Psychcentral.com

concern you and may affect you, they are still demonstrating the behavior of a pathological liar!

A pathological liar can also lie with their actions. A pathological liar may not say something which is not true, but they might decide not to correct you when you assume something that is not true. Or they may act like they know what they are doing to give you false confidence in them.

Someone renting an expensive car to impress you and persuade you to join their pyramid scheme, someone not correcting you when they hear you making a false assumption, or someone crying to get what they want, are all examples of lying with actions. If someone regularly does this, they are behaving like a pathological liar, even if they are not actively lying.

For example, my business partner would regularly act as though he knew what he was doing, and get indignant when I accused him of lying to me. In doing this he wanted to make me believe things that were not true. Just like a verbal lie, the end goal of his actions was to trick me.

Lying by omission or by action plants ideas in your head without the liar ever having to say a thing! This means they can gaslight you, because when you confront them they will easily say, "I never said that, it's all in your head", and therefore escape the confrontation.

People who regularly lie by omission or by action to make you believe false things are engaging in an activity called gaslighting. Gaslighting is when someone tries to convince you that your perception of the world is wrong. Maybe they are trying to make you doubt your senses, or your sanity. Maybe they are trying to challenge your worldview by manipulating you into following theirs. But rather than opening a debate about facts, they are simply trying to worm their way into your mind and convince you that your own judgment is poor and theirs is excellent.

Gaslighting is a particularly heinous manipulation tactic because most people do not realize it is happening. A pathological liar can gaslight you by saying, "I never said that", "you are imagining things", or "I am sure it did not happen that way". They can gaslight you by acting in a patronizing manner, or by not considering your perception and emotions, causing you to doubt yourself.[35]

The end result of living with a pathological liar can often mean either constant self-doubt, or chaos. Either they use their lies to control you, causing you to feel insecure and helpless without them, or they are completely out of control of their lying, resulting in constant consequences for them, you, and everyone in your lives.

Lesson 16: The words used by liars.

Liars tend to speak slightly different from people who are telling the truth. The three key differences between liars and honest people are: verbal diarrhea, third person use, and swearing.

Active liars are more prone than honest people to verbal diarrhea. This means they speak faster and use more words than people telling the truth. Liars using implication or omission to lie tend to do the opposite and speak much less.

Liars are more likely to speak in the third person, because they want the listener to not associate them with the lie. Liars will place blame, and even credit, on a third party, too, so that they are not seen as part of the process.

Although people who swear are more often perceived as being honest, when someone starts swearing more than usual, chances are they are lying! Again, it is thought that the energy it takes to formulate a lie distracts people from other aspects of conversation, such as norms about politeness.

These three examples hold true for many people who are lying, whether they are lying

---

[35] Dorpat, T.L. (1994) On the double whammy and gaslighting. *Psychoanalysis & Psychotherapy.* 11 pp91-96.

actively, through implication, or through omission. However, this is not always a reliable way of telling if someone is lying, as people with lower empathy may not display the same behaviors. If you do not feel guilty about saying or doing something, chances are you will not act like a guilty person. Older, more experienced liars may also be able to hide their nervousness. [36]

Exercise:

Make a point of studying speech patterns and the words used by people around you. People with lower empathy, such as narcissistic or psychopathic people, may not be very obvious liars. But someone who is more solipsistic, or Machiavellian may still display normal signs of mental exhaustion and nervousness, giving them away.

Lesson 17: The physical signs of lying.

That said, spotting a liar with reduced or absent empathy can still be very easy if you know what to look for. Most non-empathetic people display very strong physical signs that they are lying. This is because lies take place in a different part of the brain than truths.

A truth comes from our memory. This is a fairly simple process, activating only a few parts of the brain. However, hard you have to try and remember things, the actual memory will be drawn out fairly easily. This means that our body will not show many signs of stress when we tell the truth.

A lie comes from our imagination. This is a much more complicated process, activating a lot more of the brain and using a lot of oxygen. The body of a liar will display some signs of stress, even if on a personal level they are not bothered by the act of lying. We're looking for these differences.

Some signs that someone is inventing what they are saying include physical twitches, looking to their right, flushing, or licking their lips. A twitch of the hands indicates increased pulse and a rush of adrenaline. Their eye moving to the right of their face shows they are imagining

---

[36] Swol, LM.V. Et al (2011) Evidence for the Pinocchio Effect: Linguistic Differences Between Lies, Deception by Omissions, and Truths. *Official Journal for the Society for Text & Discourse, vol 49, pub 2012.*

things. Blushing and lip licking show an increase in blood pressure from the brain working harder.

Does this mean all liars show these physical signs? Again, sadly not. Some people are delusional, and therefore believe their own lies. They "remember" them in much the same way we remember truths! And some people are aware of these physical cues and have trained themselves not to show them. The vast majority of the time, a liar will display these signs.[37]

Exercise:

When you are in conversation with someone, try and analyze their posture and general behavior. Watch what they are like normally, and then when they are joking, or making things up. Telling the difference between honesty and open lies allows you to later tell when they are actually trying to deceive you.

That said, some people lie continually, and obviously these people, when caught, are not to be trusted whether or not you can see signs of lying or not.

Lesson 18: Confronting pathological liars.

Confronting a pathological liar is difficult for many reasons. For starters, many pathological liars find the truth uncomfortable. Even if the truth is not harmful to them, they are repulsed by it in almost the same way a normal person is repulsed by a lie. This could be argued to be the force of habit, like someone who cannot stand to drink clean water because they are used to soda and coffee. [38]

Sometimes the truth is uncomfortable to them because reality is not pleasant. Survivors of abuse, or people in bad relationships, will often lie about how reality works as a form of escapism. This allows them to live in a delusion which is happier, more pleasant, and more under their control than their real life. These lies act as a drug for these people and

---

[37] Kluger, J. and Masters, C. (2005) How to Spot a LIAR. *TIME August 25 2005.*

[38] Biever, C. (2005) Liars' brains make fibbing come naturally. *New Scientist. Reprint from British Journal of Psychiatry, Oct 2005.*

confronting them means taking their coping mechanism away.

Even if they do not find the truth too uncomfortable, some pathological liars will be ashamed of what they are doing. When they are caught they feel uncomfortable and angry and will double down on their lies. Being discovered is worse than being dishonest, in their mind.

If someone is using lies to manipulate you, then they will not confess to what they are doing. If you know they are liars, then you will be on your guard. This would make it harder for them to manipulate you again, so they will insist they were not lying. They might say they were telling the truth. They might say they believed it to be the truth, or that someone else lied to them first; anything but admit they were manipulating you.[39]

It can be hard to tell whether someone is lying intentionally. If you accuse someone of lying pathologically, then they could react any number of ways. A perfectly decent person who is afflicted by pathological lying may deny it vehemently, out of shame or compulsion. A manipulative person may admit to their lying, but then try and soften the blow. They may cry about it to make you pity them or insist they did not mean to hurt you. [40]

There is basically no right way to confront a pathological liar. So, what is the best solution?

According to medical professionals, the best option is just to correct them and move on. Do not trust what they say, double check every claim they make. If you catch them lying, tell them the truth, and then let them be. If they insist that what they said was true, then repeat the truth back to them again, calmly and collectedly, and let them be again.

In the case of a compulsive liar, you are sparing them the shame of being confronted. In the case of a manipulative liar, you are showing them you are not vulnerable to their attacks. And in both cases, you are psychologically arming yourself against their bad behavior. You

---

[39] Cole, T. (2001) Lying to the one you love: The use of deception in romantic relationships. *Journal of Social and Personal Relationships 18*. DePaul University.

[40] Dorpat, T.L. (1994) On the double whammy and gaslighting. *Psychoanalysis & Psychotherapy.* 11 pp91-96.

are adapting to the situation, so even if they continue to lie to you, you will be prepared. [41]

Exercise:

Practice handling liars so that you get in the habit of it. Imagine someone has lied to you and think of how you would correct them and how you would move on. For example, if someone said nobody called that day, but there is a call recorded you might say, "No, there is a call recorded," to correct them and "who was it, what did they say?" to move on.

Try this out on the following scenarios:

- You have asked a friend where they have been all day. They said "at home", but you saw them out and about.
- You said that you owed someone $100 by mistake, when you owe them $75, but they did not correct you.
- You mention a past time when a colleague lied to you, but they insist it never happened in the first place.

Lesson 19: Handling the aftermath of pathological lies.

When pathological lies are not corrected immediately, often they leave a lot of problems behind. You lose your trust in the other person, while tension and anger brews between you. It is possible that they will keep trying to push your boundaries again, to return to the routine you used to have. Not to mention, you might be placed in an uncomfortable position with other people that remain in the dark about their lies.

Exercise:

Take the same scenarios as in Lesson 16. Imagine that you did not react to these incidences of lying, and now you need to correct the aftermath. Ask yourself who you would turn to first, what you would say to them, and how you would plan your solution:

---

[41] P. Korenis, L. Gonzalez, B. Kadriu, et al. (2015) "Pseudologia fantastica: Forensic and clinical treatment implications," *Comprehensive Psychiatry, vol. 56*, pp.17-20.

- You have asked a friend where they have been all day. They said "at home", but you saw them out and about.
    - AFTERMATH: They have now started lying to you about where they are going and what they are doing, and you are not sure if they even want to spend time with you.
- You said that you owed someone $100 by mistake, when you owe them $75, but they did not correct you.
    - AFTERMATH: You move to pay them the correct amount, but they say you owed them $100.
- You are starting to talk about some pain you are experiencing, and your partner rolls their eyes.
    - AFTERMATH: You are in pain but feel you cannot tell your partner because they will not take your problems seriously.
- You mention all the work you have been doing toward a project and ask for a raise, but your manager ignores you completely.
    - AFTERMATH: Someone else gets a raise and a promotion for working on the same project. You get nothing.
- You mention a past time when a colleague lied to you, but they insist it never happened in the first place.
    - AFTERMATH: Your other coworkers now assume you are a liar, or that your memory of past events is not very reliable. They mention this incident as proof that you get things wrong.

CHAPTER THIRTEEN: THRILL-SEEKERS

A lot of Bad Guys are hardcore thrill-seekers. Whether they are diagnosed with an official mental illness, such as psychopathy or borderline personality disorder, or they are just terrible people, Bad Guys often chase a rush. They are more likely to be addicted to drugs or alcohol, to be hooked on sex or gambling or video games, to shop without considering their bank balance and spend themselves into the red. They are more likely to engage in risky behaviors like unprotected sex, extreme sports, or animal handling. They may modify their bodies, either surgically, through tattoos and piercings, or even through extreme methods such as scarification.[42]

Like with most of these behavioral problems, on its own thrill-seeking is completely harmless. Getting a tattoo does not do you, or those close to you, any harm. If you decide you want to go skydiving, then there are many ways of doing it perfectly safely, with minimal real risk. And if you are a very sexual, or otherwise physical person, there are ways of indulging carnal pleasures without opening yourself up to sexually transmitted diseases.

In fact, many of us seek thrills on some level or another in our lives. We all have our own threshold for what is "thrilling", but we like to push our limits and feel our hearts beat fast and our minds go blank at the excitement of something challenging. We are designed to live with random bursts of stress, and the relief we feel after doing something like riding a rollercoaster is deeply reviving. And, again, we are not hurting anyone by doing it.[43]

Many Bad Guys will, however, seek thrills at the expense of other people. Again, this is a case of the Bad Guy either not thinking about you, or enjoying your suffering. They do not care that you will lose money, they just want the thrill of robbing you. They do not care that you will suffer physical pain and fear, they just want the thrill of assaulting or fighting you. They do not care that they might go crazy and hurt someone, they just want the thrill of getting high or drunk. Nothing matters other than them feeling good, alive, even.

---

[42] Keller, L. and Gollwitzer, M. (2017) Mindsets Affect Risk Perception and Risk-Taking Behavior. *Social Psychology.* 48. pp135-147.

[43] Machluf, K. and Bjorklund, D.F. (2015) Understanding Risk-Taking Behavior: Insights from Evolutionary Psychology. *Emerging Trends in the Social and Behavioral Sciences.*

Bad Guys often even seek thrills at their own expense! When a Bad Guy engages in unprotected casual sex, they are putting themselves at risk of infection or pregnancy. When they take drugs, they are putting themselves at risk of arrest or physical harm. When they spend all their money in one outing, they are putting themselves at risk of ending up in debt, or on the streets. None of these things enter their consideration. All that matters to them is getting their next fix of adrenaline and dopamine.

Their addiction to thrill-seeking is precisely what makes them so dangerous. If someone is not willing to even consider their own well-being, then your well-being is completely out of their mind, too. If when they stare death in the face they just shrug, then they probably think nothing of putting your life at risk. These are exactly the sort of people who could be said to have "nothing to lose". That is not to say they do not fear punishment, only that they never even think about it so long as they are having fun.

When I was living with my shopaholic ex-girlfriend, she continually chased the next thrill. She would take my money to spend, of course which put her at risk of getting caught, arrested, and losing the relationship.

But she would also spend any money of her own, driving herself into the red, just so she could go shopping again. She never thought of the future repercussions of her actions. And if she didn't care about what happened to her, do you think she could have ever cared about what happened to me?

Sometimes thrill-seekers act criminally to get their high. My ex-girlfriend's behavior was arguably criminal because she stole from me. Domestic violence is another example of criminal thrill-seeking. It can still get worse. Some thrill-seekers will attack people, commit grand theft auto, rape, or even kill to get their thrill. Knowing that what they are doing is "forbidden" gives them the rush. The idea of getting caught is the most exciting part, and any punishment is not a deterrent, but a motivator.

Sometimes thrill-seekers will try and get a rise out of you. I have never dealt with one myself, but I have seen them in action. These are either a sort of masochist, or someone with serious delusions of grandeur. They are trying to get you to argue with them, shout at them, or physically attack them. If they are doing this because they are masochists, or have a victim complex, they want to be seen to suffer. If they are doing it because they believe they are untouchable, they will then retaliate against you. Usually, their reactions will be completely disproportionate to your original action.[44]

Sometimes thrill-seekers will lie repeatedly for the rush. Again, it is the knowledge they are doing something forbidden which motivates them. Sometimes they relish the idea of getting caught and being challenged. This connects them to the thrill-seekers who want to get a rise out of you. But often thrill-seekers who lie do so because they believe they will never be caught. It gives them a rush to think that they are somehow better than you. "Tricking" their victims are their top priority, and doing so makes them feel intelligent, educated, or important. [45]

Sometimes thrill-seekers will simply adopt harmful habits without considering you. They are not trying to hurt you, make you angry, or trick you. They are managing to avoid engaging in criminal behaviors. Do not be fooled as they are still taking serious risks. Maybe they are getting drunk every single day and wrecking their health. Maybe they are playing with knives or fire, making sure to avoid harming others, but hurting themselves. Maybe they are spending all their own money and ending up in serious debt.[46]

Whatever they are doing, it is destroying *them* not *you*, so they think it is okay. What they don't realize is that everything they do influences your life. The alcoholic does not see that you need to pay for their medical bills, or nurse them back to health. The pyromaniac does not see that you would need to arrange their funeral. The shopaholic does not see that you will have to support them when they are homeless.

---

[44] Laurene, K.R. (2010) Risky Living: A comparison of criminal risk-taking and risk perception in adolescent and young adult nonoffenders and offenders. Bowling Green State University.

[45] Cole, T. (2001) Lying to the one you love: The use of deception in romantic relationships. *Journal of Social and Personal Relationships 18.* DePaul University.

[46] Machluf, K. and Bjorklund, D.F. (2015) Understanding Risk-Taking Behavior: Insights from Evolutionary Psychology. *Emerging Trends in the Social and Behavioral Sciences.*

Not to mention the mental and emotional pain they cause. Almost every thrill-seeker of every type will completely ignore the mental and emotional pain they are putting you through. At best, they will tell you to "get over it". At worst, they cannot understand why you care. They will probably never see things through your eyes and stop hurting you.[47]

The end result of all these behaviors is that they are continually putting their lives, health, money, safety, and relationships at risk. And if you are connected to them, they may also be putting *your* life, health, money, safety, and relationships at risk! Whether they are your partner, your parent, your child, your friend, or your coworker, you are on some level responsible for them.

When anything they do backfires, you might find out you have a legal responsibility to help them. Or you might find you are emotionally drawn to helping them. Or you may be pressured by your community into helping them. Whatever the case, their behavior puts your well-being at risk.

Another rarely discussed aspect of handling Bad Guys is that sometimes victims seek out Bad Guys because *the victim* is a thrill-seeker. There are some people who crave the thrills of a risky relationship because it makes them feel alive, sexually aroused, or simply not bored. When there is not a Bad Guy in their lives, they may feel lonely, bored, or aimless.

In many ways this is because they have fallen into the habit of abuse. In much the same way as widows and empty nesters find it hard to adapt to life after losing someone, victims may find it hard to adapt to life without their abuser. They are so used to living in fear, that when they are not afraid they feel empty. Confusing fear for excitement, they seek another Bad Guy to fill the void.[48]

Many Bad Guy behaviors can trigger the rush which a thrill-seeker loves. Physical violence

---

[47] Machluf, K. and Bjorklund, D.F. (2015) Understanding Risk-Taking Behavior: Insights from Evolutionary Psychology. *Emerging Trends in the Social and Behavioral Sciences.*

[48] Whitaker DJ, Haileyesus T, Swahn M, Saltzman LS. (2007) Differences in frequency of violence and reported injury between relationships with reciprocal and nonreciprocal intimate partner violence. *Am J Public Health 97: pp941 - 947*

may make a masochist feel sexually aroused, or someone with a martyr complex feel validated. Gaslighting and lying may provide arguments which a thrill-seeker may enjoy. Narcissistic self-love and a delusional sense of grandeur can give a thrill-seeker a power struggle which can provide regular excitement. Some victims of Bad Guys will not only seek out Bad Guys to have relationships with, but will actively provoke them, as they do not feel happy unless they are in an aggressive relationship.

This push and pull of baiting and abuse is a dangerous game. Out of the 24% of relationships with domestic violence, half of them are reciprocally violent, meaning that both parties are equally as violent to one another. Because in a reciprocally violent relationship both partners are baiting *and* abusing, reciprocally violent relationships have the highest rate of injury among all domestic violence situations at 31.4%.[49]

Lesson 20: Avoiding thrill-seekers.

If you are a perfectly ordinary person, it can be easy to become swept up in the exciting life of a thrill-seeker. Someone heavily tattooed who drinks excessively, has wild sex, and practices combat sports is our Hollywood-movie-definition of someone fun, interesting, and thrilling. And not all thrill-seekers cause anyone any harm. Most of them are perfectly happy to get a tattoo and go to boxing classes.

It is important to spot the difference between a healthy thrill-seeker and a taker of unnecessary risks. Many people are what you would call adrenaline junkies. They will do things which we consider highly dangerous just for the rush. As long as they are doing it with all available safety measures, and as long as it is legal and does not put anyone else at risk, they are still normal people.

Even if you end up taking care of their injuries, bills, or other issues, if you do this willingly sometimes it is not a problem. Some people genuinely do not mind taking on some extra work to care for their loved ones. And if you discussed this in advance and they are staying within agreed limits, that is up to you as individuals.

---

[49] McQueen, D. (2011) Domestic violence is most commonly reciprocal. *The Psychiatrist.* Royal College of Psychiatrists.

Even if you cannot decide how much risk is too much, you might wisely decide to make criminal activity a hard boundary for you. Many Bad Guys seem to believe they are untouchable because the police haven't caught them yet. No matter how much risk-taking behavior you accept from them, do not overlook criminal behavior. This could not only affect their whole life, but it may affect yours. You are at risk of being a victim of one of their crimes or considered an accomplice. Being a grass is better than being hurt or arrested.

Exercise:

Try and decide whether the thrill-seekers in your life are healthy or dangerous. Like with sadists, there are a few simple questions that should help you reach a conclusion:

1. Do they avoid behaviors which are criminal, or which actively harm nonconsenting parties?
2. Do they talk to you openly and honestly about their thrills?
3. Do they make use of all available safety measures, insurance, etc.?
4. Do they ask for your consent before involving you in their thrill-seeking?
5. Do they acknowledge your fears and feelings as valid, even if they continue to thrill-seek safely afterwards?

If you can answer "yes" to all these questions, then this person is just an adrenaline junkie. If you answer "maybe" or "no" to any of these questions, there may be a problem in your relationship. But if you answer "no" to all these questions, then you are dealing with someone who is not considering your well-being at all.

Lesson 21: Finding healthy thrills.

If you find you keep going back to negative relationships because you miss the excitement, you may be a thrill-seeker yourself. Chasing thrills in bad relationships can be a hard habit to break, and you may feel lost, confused, and bored without a Bad Guy to give you trouble.

You need to find ways of indulging that need for excitement without putting yourself in harm's way. Many people find that an adrenaline-packed hobby provides them with that same feeling in a safer environment. Martial arts, skydiving, shooting, mountain biking, or rafting might help you burn off some steam, boost your dopamine, and keep your brain busy.

Other people find that it is the intimate aggression they crave the most. These people are most likely masochists, and, as we have already explored, it is possible to indulge your masochism in a safe, loving relationship. You need to find a sadistic partner who understands boundaries, loves and respects you, and keeps the aggression to the bedroom. With them, you can explore different ways of providing the thrill you crave.

Exercise:

Look into different ways of enjoying an exciting personal life without having to deal with Bad Guys every day. Ask yourself whether you crave the arguments, the tension, the physical activity, or the physical aggression. Depending on your specific needs, find a healthy, safe alternative which does not put you at risk.

CHAPTER FOURTEEN: PSYCHOS, BORDERLINES, CODEPENDENCE - MENTAL HEALTH AND TOXIC RELATIONSHIPS

Many people put Bad Guy behavior down to mental illness. This may seem logical at first. After all, Bad Guys tend to act in ways that are irrational, dangerous, and poorly empathetic. And it is a comforting to think that the person is ill as opposed to being inherently bad. It is reassuring to tell ourselves, "These people are not like that on purpose, they are not *truly* bad, they are just damaged. They don't know what they are doing. They are broken and malfunctioning, like a computer with a virus."

Unfortunately, this is a simplification. As we have seen over the course of this book, Bad Guy behaviors are just that: behaviors. You don't need to be a narcissist to act narcissistic, or a psychopath to act psychopathic. Plenty of Bad Guys have nothing clinically wrong with them at all.

Think of it this way: If you have a fever, a sore throat, a persistent sneeze, a headache, and are tired, you probably have a cold. But if you have a headache, would you assume you had a cold? What about if you had a headache and are tired? Just because we have some of the symptoms of an illness does not mean we have the illness. Likewise, just because a person has some symptoms of a mental illness does not mean they have the illness![50]

They might still be a Bad Guy. They might still be dangerous, a bad influence, etc. But they are not mentally ill. They are just terrible people, pure and simple.

Nevertheless, sometimes a collection of these Bad Guy behaviors *does* come together to form a clinically diagnosed mental illness. And some mental illnesses are more common among Bad Guys than others.

Just as it is important to acknowledge that not all Bad Guys are mentally ill, it is important

---

[50] CurtinLife (2017) Identifying mental health problems and conditions. Curtin University. Curtin.edu.au

to acknowledge that some mental illnesses give rise to a plethora of Bad Guys. By acknowledging this and learning how to spot the warning signs of these mental illnesses, we can then go on to learn how to handle people with these disorders. Consider it a sort of shortcut to understanding specific groups of Bad Guys.

Psychopathy or antisocial personality disorder

Psychopaths, as defined by the DSM V, are possibly one of the most dangerous Bad Guys, and one of the mental illnesses where almost every sufferer ends up being a Bad Guy. Because they are characterized by a lack of empathy, compulsive lying, sadistic tendencies, thrill-seeking behavior, and no concern for law and order, they are very prone to ruining their lives and those of others. And their lack of remorse means you can't do anything to convince them to stop ruining lives. Either they decide it is in their own best interests to be good, or they will be a Bad Guy forever.

Narcissism

Narcissists, as we have already discussed, are another very troublesome group. They are self-obsessed, prone to lying, have little to no empathy, and are often so unemotional that they are unable to relate on any level to other people. Unlike psychopaths they are not quite so impulsive. If they can be persuaded it is in their own best interests to be good, they will almost always behave themselves. If they are very solipsistic, however, it would be very hard to get through to them, as they cannot on any level understand that other people have their own needs and interests. A narcissist with a high level of solipsism will probably always be a Bad Guy.

Borderline personality disorder

A condition we have not yet discussed in detail, borderline personality disorder is overlooked by most, and gets a bad rap by those that notice it. People with borderline personality disorder are terrified of being abandoned, have great difficulty forming healthy relationships, are highly impulsive, prone to self-harm, and alternate between inappropriately intense emotion and completely lacking emotion. Because of this they are very prone to reckless behavior which puts themselves and others at risk. Many of their victims consider them to be as dangerous as psychopaths or narcissists, which is actually not true. That said, their impulsivity and emotional instability make them prone to many Bad

Guy behaviors. They are best avoided.

Codependency

Codependent people are usually considered victims rather than perpetrators because sufferers of codependency usually seek out and attach themselves to people with any of the other five mental health conditions listed here. When in these relationships, they are often victimized and abused, which is not acceptable. Even when in a relationship with a normal, healthy person, someone with codependency still behaves in a way which may be dangerous to the other party. They can be emotionally volatile, manipulative, and thrill-seeking to a point of harming themselves and others. If they do not control these behaviors, they are bound to be a Bad Guy.[51]

Schizoid personality disorder

People with schizoid personality disorder, as defined by the DSM V, are unable to maintain a normal and healthy relationship with normal and healthy people. They are characterized by a lack of interest in any close relationships, even family, emotional detachment, lack of pleasure in life that does not stem from depression, indifference to praise or criticism, few hobbies or interests, and shallow affect. They are another type that does not set out to harm you, but which hurts you with indifference. They do not notice or care when they are hurting you, which can make them Bad Guys.

Histrionic personality disorder

People with histrionic personality disorder are a sort of horrible combination of the worst elements of a narcissist and a psychopath. Under the DSM V definition, they are wholly self-centered, obsessed with appearances and being loved, incredibly gullible, very dramatic and attention-seeking, and impulsive to a point of harming themselves and others to get their own way. They could therefore be argued to be the most extreme form of solipsist. Because they live in their own little bubble where nothing matters except being popular, they will often hurt others. Unless they can be shown that they get better attention for being good,

---

[51] Brandes Hillborg, V.L. (1995) The Relationship Between the Level of Codependent Behavior and the Level of Differentiation of Self Among Nursing Students.

they will be a Bad Guy.[52]

Some people with these conditions are perfectly nice people. Some psychopaths are able to control themselves and lead normal lives away from others. Some narcissists use benevolence to fuel their ego. Some borderlines work hard to control their behavior. Some codependent people seek supportive relationships full of love and trust. Some schizoid people seek relationships with others like themselves where they do no harm. Some histrionic people seek attention with grand acts of kindness.

Most people with these conditions will, however, fall into the category of Bad Guy. If every day you are battling with impulsivity, self-obsession, or paranoia, eventually you are going to crack. And, in most cases, the punishment for indulging their disorder is less painful than having to repress it every single day.

This internal suffering does not justify their behavior. And it doesn't mean you have to put up with it, but it *does* explain their reasoning for hurting others. To you or me it would require effort to be so selfish, reckless, and paranoid we wreck someone's life. To them, it is a huge effort *not* to ruin lives.

Some people with other psychological conditions may be at risk of becoming Bad Guys but are not automatically Bad Guys. In fact, most people with these conditions are perfectly healthy, functional people. They may be a little bit difficult to deal with every day, but they mean no harm and often make an earnest effort to act as normally as possible.

Bipolar disorder

Bipolar disorder actually refers to a spectrum of disorders characterized by mood swings that are *not* a natural emotional reaction to a situation. It ranges from dysthymia, where sufferers experience flat moods followed by mild depression, all the way to Bipolar I, where sufferers experience clinical depression followed by extreme mania. Even though these mood swings can be intense, they are the main trait of the disorder and can usually be

---

52 American Psychiatric Association. (2013). Diagnostic and statistical manual of mental disorders (5th ed.).

managed with medication and therapy.

Asperger Syndrome

Asperger Syndrome is a form of autism where the individual is unable to interact on a natural, social level, but is otherwise quite normal. In the DSM V Asperger Syndrome has been merged with other forms of autism into Autism Spectrum Disorder. They are able to communicate clearly, hold jobs, and even understand others most of the time. However, they have great difficulty reading nonverbal communication, tone of voice, or emotions, which can make it seem as though they do not care or are being hostile. Usually, if you communicate a bit more directly they are wonderful people to be around.

Schizophrenia

Schizophrenia refers to a wide range of disorders characterized by having many serious psychiatric symptoms, like paranoia, hallucinations, obsessions, etc. Because schizophrenics are often detached from reality, they can become easily confused or agitated, making them hostile toward others. They can also act highly impulsively and are prone to risk-taking. Most of the time schizophrenia can be treated with antipsychotic drugs, making the sufferer much more functional.

Major depressive disorder

Major depressive disorder is also known as clinical depression. Contrary to popular belief, depression is not just "feeling sad". In fact, many sufferers feel nothing at all, or feel angry during their depressive episodes. Depression causes a huge range of symptoms, from lethargy and exhaustion, to memory loss, to muscle aches and nerve pain. When a person goes through a depressive episode, their brain becomes much less active, causing trouble thinking, remembering, and learning. These episodes can last anywhere from a few hours to a lifetime. Although people with depression may be a little blunt, rude, or short-tempered, generally they are pleasant people who wish you no harm.

Post-Traumatic Stress Disorder

PTSD is most commonly associated with people who have witnessed death and devastation at war or in a criminal environment, or who have been tortured. The reality is that anyone can get PTSD, and not just from witnessing or experiencing death and torture. It can be caused by verbal abuse, the loss of a loved one, a traumatic childhood, etc. PTSD is characterized by reliving the traumatic event, an intense need to avoid things that remind them of their trauma, being anxious and easily alarmed, and depression symptoms. A person with PTSD may be quick to anger or may react disproportionately to things you consider normal. However, outside of their triggers they are very normal, balanced people.[53]

Most of these people, as mentioned, are not automatically bad people. They might do bad things because of their condition. The difference between these five and the six conditions prone to Bad Guys is that these five are not ruled by a symptom that makes them hurt others. Being depressed, easily scared, or confused, does not make you dangerous. Being impulsive, paranoid, and self-centered does.

Does this mean that people with these five conditions *can't* be Bad Guys? Of course not! Every type of person can be a Bad Guy. In fact, just because you have one mental health condition does not mean you cannot have others. Someone who is bipolar could easily also be antisocial, or someone with PTSD could be borderline. It is important to bear in mind that not all mental health conditions make people act in a way that harms others, and that sometimes someone with a condition may hurt others accidentally, but overall still be a good person to be around.

Lesson 22: Dealing with a diagnosed mental health condition.

When someone in your life suffers from a diagnosed mental health condition, it can be hard not to leap to conclusions. With free access to the internet, and so many pseudo-professionals on TV, all of us would like to think we know a little bit about mental illness. But real mental health conditions are not as simple as a health website entry, or a news report, or a TV character.

People are very varied. Even people with the same mental health condition can be completely different in how it manifests. Of two people with Bipolar II, one may be on medication and the other may self-manage, one may be prone to anger and the other to flat moods, one may

---

[53] American Psychiatric Association. (2013). Diagnostic and statistical manual of mental disorders (5th ed.).

be more lethargic and the other more paranoid, and both will have unique thoughts, interests, and lives. Just because you know someone's diagnosis does not mean you know all about them.

When you find out about someone's diagnosed mental health condition, take a step back. Unless the person suffers from one of the six conditions most prone to Bad Guys, there is no reason to assume they will harm you. There is also no reason to assume they need your help or want to change either. Most people with diagnosed mental health conditions are receiving support and treatment and are functional members of society.

Nevertheless, it is important to adapt to ensure everyone's safety. Most people with mental health conditions will want to warn you well in advance to prepare you for any complications. Make the most of this opportunity to learn all about them and their experience of the condition.

Exercise:

If there is anyone important in your life with a diagnosed mental health condition, sit down with them and talk to them about it. The more you know about their condition and the better you understand them, the better protected both of you will be. Consider asking them:

1. What is it like having your condition?
2. Are there any times you are worried you might harm yourself or others?
3. What can I do to help?
4. Is there anything important I need to know?

At first you are going to have to trust what they say. Unless you are a psychiatrist, you will not be able to diagnose them yourself, or second-guess their claims. Use your best judgment. If it seems they are a pathological liar, you might need to have this conversation with other people in their lives and get to the truth of the matter.

It is also important to use this time to determine if this person is a Bad Guy, or at risk of becoming a Bad Guy. Sometimes, learning about someone's mental health condition helps you learn how to change your behavior to protect them. Or it might tell you to walk away and never see them again. If they display Bad Guy attitudes or behaviors, and are also diagnosed with a mental health condition, you do not have to stay.

It is not your responsibility to be nice to them. It is not your responsibility to help them. It is not your responsibility to change them. You need to look after yourself and your loved ones.

CHAPTER FIFTEEN: ISN'T IT SELFISH TO LOOK OUT FOR MYSELF?

A lot of people experience difficulties when it comes to looking after their own interests. Usually, this manifests as giving up your time, money, or energy for others. In fact, most of us will engage in self-sacrificing behavior some of the time, and this altruism is a natural, healthy human behavior. We do not *need* all the time and money we have. We cannot fill our whole day with self-serving activities. So, we give a little bit to others, they give back, and slowly we build communities that maintain all of civilization.

The problem arises when the altruism goes too far. You probably know someone who sacrifices everything for others. Who gets ill from overworking themselves. Who gives away so much of their money that they have to budget carefully. Who never denies anyone their time. Who feels bad for refusing even a single request. This may even be you! And although this behavior comes from the right place, it is an unhealthy response to a bad environment, which will slowly break you down. This is actually known as pathological altruism.[54]

Most of us deeply care about those close to us, and about society in general. Even when we show ourselves no love, we want other humans to be happy. We probably even want our Bad Guys to be happy! So even when we have given up on looking after ourselves, we aim to do right by other people.[55] The problem with that philosophy is that you can't just keep looking after other people and not look after yourself. You need to eat, to rest, to have fun, to socialize. And if you don't, you get ill. And if you are ill, how can you help anyone else?

Just like the airplane message that tells you to, "attach your mask before assisting others", you need to make sure you are in good shape before you can help anyone! Because if you give away all your money, there is no money to give. If you use up all your time, you have no time to stay healthy. If you burn all your energy, you end up ill and relying on other people instead. The people who depend on you also need you to look after yourself.

---

[54] Oakley, B. (2012) *Pathological Altruism.* Oxford University Press.
[55] Keltner, D. (2014) The Compassionate Instinct. *Big Ideas – Greater Good Magazine.* UC Berkeley

Most importantly, you are the only person who can always look out for you! Nobody else lives inside your head. Nobody else is always by your side, so nobody else can keep an eye out and make sure you are safe from negative influences. You need to keep Bad Guys out of your life, push them away when they try and worm into your circles, turn down their requests, and avoid their toxic and abusive behavior. You need to defend yourself.

If you never defend yourself, then one of two things will happen. If you are lucky enough to never be alone with a Bad Guy, you are putting pressure on others to protect you. Bad Guys are everywhere. To always avoid them, you rely on friends, family, law enforcement, etc., to always keep an eye out and make sure they never reach you. This does the opposite of what you want. It doesn't make you independent, it makes you a burden to the people you want to help!

If, like most of us, you *do* encounter a Bad Guy at some point, tread with caution. You might need to defend yourself, or Bad Guys will be tempted to take advantage. This isn't right, but it's better to protect yourself in the beginning than be sorry later.

Which means you need to value yourself and your own worth. It is not impossible to look after something you place no value on, but it is very difficult. We already know that a mother can lift cars to save her baby, but that many people can't even get out of bed for a job they don't like. Similarly, if we do not value ourselves and love ourselves, how can we make the effort to look after ourselves?

In extreme cases where an individual does not love themselves we can see depressed people who manage to look after others yet forget to shower or even eat. Even the simplest of self-care stops happening when you do not think you deserve it.[56]

This is especially true if you have had some negative experiences with Bad Guys! For starters, if you have been around a Bad Guy they may have attacked your self-worth. Children,

---

[56] Oakley, B. (2012) *Pathological Altruism.* Oxford University Press.

parents, and partners of narcissists, for example, often report feeling as though the narcissist is a very important person, meanwhile, they feel worthless. This happens because the Bad Guy is so overconfident in their own superiority, that you start to believe it yourself. [57]

There is also an element of Stockholm Syndrome. This is a condition where victims are trapped and begin to empathize with their abusers. They may eventually conclude that the abuser is also a victim, or that it is them versus the world. Most sufferers of Stockholm Syndrome correctly identify the abuser when they are no longer in the environment. But even then, the sensation of disorientation, loss of identity, and low self-esteem can persist.[58]

As the cherry on top, when you are around a Bad Guy it can make you feel as though certain behaviors are just Bad Guy behaviors and must be avoided. You may respect yourself, you may know that the Bad Guy was a terrible person, but you start throwing the baby out with the bathwater. You identify "keeping my money", "refusing to help", or "having a sick day from work" as Bad Guy behaviors and commit to never doing them. In that sense, it is a bit like PTSD. Even when there are times when saving money, turning down a request, and having a sick day are perfectly reasonable, you feel an instinctive revulsion, panic, or anger at the mere thought.[59]

A lot of territory lies between "not loving yourself" and "being self-centered". You can look out for yourself without being selfish and without hurting others.

Throughout this book we have observed many Bad Guy behaviors and seen how they come together to hurt others. In almost every case we have also seen how these behaviors are a natural part of being human. Just because the extreme form of a behavior is bad does not taint the whole spectrum. Moving closer to the Bad Guys' end of the spectrum is not a wicked thing to do. In fact, it could be said that *both* extremes are bad, and that wherever you are on the spectrum you should be moving toward the center. Which means if you have no self-

---

[57] Hill, K.S. (1998) Perceived abuse: Correlation with self-esteem and educational success. *ScholarWorks at University of Montana.*

[58] Yoo, D. (2014) Stockholm Syndrome Explained by the Stanford Prison Experiment. *The nerve blog.*

[59] Lorenz, B. (2013) How Bullied Children Grow into Wounded Adults. *Education – Greater Good Magazine.* UC Berkeley

love, self-respect, or self-esteem, you need to work on building some.

It is important to look for and recognize your flaws. We need to always be focused on becoming better people, but it is equally important to build your self-esteem. You need to be able to look at yourself, see your flaws, and still love yourself. Even if that means putting your interests before someone else's.

Lesson 23: Your self-esteem.

Self-love is when you care for yourself in much the same way you would care for a child, pet, or partner. You make sure you are fed, safe, rested, and happy. Most people experience some level of self-love. Very few people do not love themselves at all. However, we all love ourselves in different ways, and to different extents. Most people also experience self-love that could be improved because they esteem themselves too lowly.

The scale of self-esteem ranges from "no self-esteem" to "delusions of godliness", with very many stages falling in between. They can be summarized with the following statements:

0.0: I have no value at all and nobody values me.

0.1: I matter to some people, but not to myself.

0.25: I have no intrinsic value, but things I do can add value to me.

0.4: I am below average.

0.5: I am no greater and no lesser than anyone else.

0.6: I am above average.

0.75: I am intrinsically more important than others, but I must work for it.

0.9: I am better than everyone else.

1.0: I am a God.

It could be said that the healthy range of self-esteem ranges from 0.4-0.6, or from 0.25-0.75 if you are willing to consider slightly disordered people to still be healthy. Many people who have a self-esteem at or below 0.25 fear becoming a person with a self-esteem of 0.75-1.0.

But looking at the scale, we can see how that is ridiculous. A slight increase would do these people, and the world, more good than harm![60]

Exercise:

Try and place yourself on the scale of self-esteem. Where do you fall? Why do you think this is? If you fear that you have been deeply hurt by interactions with Bad Guys, or that you are suffering depression, you might benefit from therapy sessions to help you get to the root of your low self-esteem.

Lesson 24: Developing a habit of self-love.

As mentioned earlier, self-love is an action, not just a feeling. Self-love is when you do things to make sure you are healthy and happy. If, like most people, you often if not always put others before yourself, you need to ask yourself how you can self-love a little more.

Once you have already achieved a healthy self-esteem, you might find that your life in many ways needs overhauling to encourage you to love yourself more. You will probably find that you are depriving yourself in many ways, but that there is no time in your day to make up for it. If you regularly go hungry at lunchtime, you need to practice effective time management, and make lunch a part of your routine. If you overwork yourself and are tired, you need to determine what you can get rid of to look after yourself.[61]

Exercise:

It is important to take time to evaluate our lives and relationships in an unstressed environment. Find a nice, quiet place to meditate on your life and circumstances. Try and work out what elements of your life are using the most time, money, and energy. See which ones could be eliminated or could be changed to take up less time. There are bound to be things you can sacrifice to make time for yourself.

---

[60] Silber, E. and Tippett, Jean (1965) "Self-esteem: Clinical assessment and measurement validation." *Psychological Reports, 16, 1017-1071*

[61] Blascovich, J., and Tomaka, J. (1993) "Measures of Self-Esteem." *Measures of Personality and Social Psychological Attitudes.* Third Edition. Ann Arbor: Institute for Social Research Pp. 115-160

Often this will involve turning other people down! You will have to tell your boss that you can't take on more work. You will have to tell your mother to call you some other time. You will have to let your kids skip a day of swimming class. You will have to step back and say, "I need to look after myself." This is not easy, but most normal, healthy people will understand and will make room for you to self-love.

On the flip side, we have the Bad Guys, who will not take kindly to our efforts to look after something that is not them!

CHAPTER SIXTEEN: CULTIVATING OUTCOME INDEPENDENCE

When we begin trying to love ourselves, we find out the true colors of many people in our lives. People who love us will be genuinely pleased for us, and glad to see us looking after ourselves. People who want us to focus on them will become jealous or confused. They will not notice that we are happier or healthier. They will just see we are robbing them of *their* time with us, *their* free labor, and *their* handouts. They may even play the victim, trying to make you pity them, and making you feel like a terrible person for daring to reject them.[62]

As the Bad Guys crawl out of the woodwork, all of them will be bitter. Like a vulture who waits for an animal to die, they are disappointed to see their "meal" getting up and walking away! If their attempts to provoke pity do not work, they will react in one of two ways next.

Some Bad Guys will retreat to lick their wounds. These Bad Guys are usually either not massively invested in the relationship because they have something else to turn to or realize that it is a losing battle and is not worth their time. Unfortunately, many Bad Guys will feel an intense desire for revenge. This vindictiveness, if not handled properly, can ruin lives.

A Bad Guy, when rejected, has an almost limitless number of tools to bully you with, ranging from petty to criminal. They might spread rumors about you, to put other people off dating you or socializing with you. They might torment other people in your life to drive them away from you. They might damage your property. They might try and get your employer to fire you. They might even physically attack you. All of these are ways of trying to "territory mark" you, to let you, and everyone else, know you are "theirs".[63]

Outcome independence is the only real way of fighting this vindictiveness. We want to be at a stage in our lives where it doesn't matter whose bridge we have to burn, or what they try to do to us, we will still pick ourselves up and keep on going. This is much easier said than done. How do you get to a point in your life where someone wanting to punch you, calling

---

[62] Abuse Hurts. (2009) Barriers to Leaving. University of Michigan.

[63] Fleury, R.E. Et al (2000) When Ending the Relationship Doesn't End the Violence: Women's Experiences of Violence by Former Partners. *Violence Against Women, Vol 6, no 12, Dec 2000.*

your employer to spread rumors about you, or stalking your new partner, does not bother you?

But outcome independence is a two-step process. We cannot be emotionally independent from someone if they are able to physically hurt us! It is impossible to be outcome independent of a tiger in your front room. You need to make sure you are personally and physically *safe* before you change your attitude.

Therefore, the first step to outcome independence is not to put others in control of our lives! When I let my ex-girlfriend live with me, I was giving her power over me. When I allowed my business partner to manage his side of the business, I put him in control of my money.

Whatever you do in life, you do not want to allow other people to have the option of hurting you. It is not paranoid to have all tenants on the lease, it is protecting you if they decide to skip paying rent. It is not cruel to refuse a loan to someone with a gambling problem, it is reasonable. It is not wrong to take out a restraining order against someone who was violent to you, it is responsible. Most people who fear these things are the people who wanted to take advantage of you.

When we are physically independent, we face the even bigger hurdle of emotional independence. Most of us connect on an emotional level to the people in our lives, even if they have not connected with us. Many people have friends, relatives, coworkers, or partners who are Bad Guys, and deeply love them. Life would not be so easy for Bad Guys if they were not able to create an emotional bond! [64]

From the moment a relationship begins, we need to remind ourselves that the other party is human. Throughout an entire relationship, we should not give people free passes on Bad Guy behavior, even if they are close friends, relatives, or romantic partners. Again, it might seem a little over the top at first, but this is nothing radical. All you need to do is treat everyone equally, and make sure your own interests are not repeatedly cast aside for anyone

---

[64] Boulette, T. R. & Andersen, S. M. (1986). "Mind control" and the battering of women. *The Cultic Studies Journal, 3,* 25-34.

else.

When we first meet people, we need to vet, vet, vet. We need to pay attention to how this new person treats others. If they are a Bad Guy to other people, chances are they will be a Bad Guy to us, too. But don't go by word of mouth alone. We need to watch their actions and words, rather than trust their reputation. We need to see if they are honest, kind, and emotionally balanced before putting our trust in them.

It can be easy to assume the best of everyone, but that is what Bad Guys count on. Vetting, again, is not extreme or cruel. Most people will pass our vetting with flying colors! Most people will demonstrate that they are honest, kind, and emotionally balanced, making them wonderful people to be around. Only a select few will need to be avoided.[65]

We should also not be needing to fight to win someone over. No matter how "absolutely fantastic" someone is, we should not try and have a relationship with someone who is not interested in socializing with us. Nor should we begin a relationship by putting someone on a pedestal. If the relationship does not begin with everyone on equal footing, showing mutual interest in one another, it does not need to be "fought for". Just let it go. Look for people who find you interesting and pleasant, people who are just as interested in you as you are in them.[66]

Even in a relationship of equals, where the other party has proven they are decent, it is important to establish boundaries. When relationships begin, we cannot afford to be "lovesick". This happens often, and not just in romantic relationships, but in friendships, family relationships, and even work relationships.

Lovesickness is related to wanting to "win them over". We are so desperate to make a good impression and receive praise that we will allow people to do things nobody else is allowed to do. We will do things we are not comfortable doing. Then, we feel we cannot take these

---

[65] Baker, A. (1997) Abusive relationships often start with manipulation. *NewsNet Staff Writer.* BYU School of Communications.

[66] Gordon, A.M. (2012) When Are You Sacrificing Too Much in Your Relationship? *Relationships – Greater Good Magazine.* UC Berkeley

permissions back. It is important to set healthy boundaries from the onset, but even if you did not set boundaries, or you are not comfortable with your boundaries, it is never too late to redefine them.

It can help to sit down with someone and talk to them about the nature of your relationship, but you can also define your boundaries more casually. When they say something that offends you, you can ask them to please not say that around you, and maybe explain why. If they ask you to do something, you can always turn them down, no matter how many times you did it before. A normal person will respect your boundaries and aim to make you happy.

You should also encourage them to express themselves openly and make their own boundaries clear. If they look uncomfortable, ask why and try and avoid repeating your behavior. If they do not want to do something, make it very clear they do not have to. Create a healthy, communicative environment for your relationship to grow.

Establishing boundaries is not the same as building a wall! When we build walls, we are actively excluding people in the first place. We are sending out a message that we are not open to relationships. On the other hand, boundaries are established as the relationship progresses. A wall says, "I cannot be friends with a member of your faith", a boundary says, "I would rather not discuss faith with you".

No matter what stage our relationship is at, we must defend these boundaries. Our outcome independence relies on us having an independent life, and a healthy attitude toward the people in it. If we allow them to push past our boundaries and break our rules, we open ourselves up to being hurt, physically or emotionally. Normal, healthy people will not do this to us. But everyone can potentially be a Bad Guy, so we need to take these basic precautions just in case. A healthy person will understand our boundaries and respect them.

And when relationships come to an end, for whatever reason, we need to again establish our boundaries. There will be new boundaries, whether the relationship transforms or ends completely. You might ask them not to talk to you, or to avoid certain subjects. You might ask for your possessions back, or to stop having your usual coffee date. Whatever they are, define your new boundaries clearly and discuss them with the other party.[67]

There is no reason why every relationship should end on a sour note, and nobody should *ever* leave you feeling fearful for your own well-being at any point in a relationship. As your life changes and transforms, so much the people in it. And if you are outcome independent, then you have nothing to fear.

Lesson 25: Who are the Bad Guys in your life?

Having completed this book, the time has come to really scrutinize your relationships with others. You might find it suddenly really easy to spot Bad Guys around you, but not to notice the ones in your own social circles! As we have already discussed, we tend to give the benefit of the doubt to people we know. We will try and use any aspect of their lives to justify their behavior.

At the end of the day, it comes back to what we discussed at the very start of this book. Bad Guys are the ones who are harming you. Having explored your own life and found areas where you could show yourself a little more love, you have probably discovered some people who are enormous time and energy sinks. Maybe they are very demanding. Or very inconsiderate. Maybe we value them ridiculously highly for no reasonable motive. Some of them might accept it with good grace when we say, "I'm sorry I can't help. I need to take care of myself." But others will get angry.

When it comes to people who are eating up all our time, the answer is simple. Either they step back and let us look after ourselves, or they are a Bad Guy. No matter what excuses they (or you!) conjure up, they are bad for you, and they need to be gone.

Exercise:

To find the Bad Guys, you will need to use all the tools in this book. You will need to not only look out for the obvious signs, but also for subtle clues that someone is trying to use you. And it is important to start with the people you already know!

---

67 University Counseling Service. (2017) Boundaries in Relationships. University of Iowa.

Look at the people who are using up most of your time, energy, and money on a day to day basis. Ask yourself whether they need so much from you. Ask *them* whether they need so much from you. If you feel they are taking advantage of you, and they feel they are being reasonable, you might need to consider cutting ties with them, for your own well-being. You cannot reach a balanced agreement with someone whose perspective is so focused on taking advantage of you.

Exercise:

Cutting ties with Bad Guys is not easy. Just because they are bad does not mean we do not feel guilt upon leaving them behind. We will remember good times with them. We will feel good things for them. We will want to make sure that they are well and happy. And sometimes this cannot be.

Sometimes people will get angry or sad when we cut ties with them. They might threaten you, other people, or themselves to try and get you back. The more important you were to them, emotionally or as a source of money and labor, the more of a fight they will put up. You need to make sure that you are safe, and they are safe. Contact relevant services if you are scared they will hurt themselves or others. Get a restraining order if they have been criminally abusive.

And finally, do not give in and go back. If you have put all the time and energy and thought into ending this relationship, it was for a reason. They will try and bait you back. You may see things through rose-tinted glasses after creating distance. Don't be fooled. The reality is that the relationship hurt you, and now it is not. You need to stay strong and look after yourself and your loved ones first and foremost.

CONCLUSION

To wrap up this important material, I feel it is important to note that it is not your fault if you have allowed Bad Guys into your life until now. You may have been hurt by them physically or emotionally, lost faith in humanity, been robbed, dismissed, and ostracized. This is not your fault.

Where victims of abuse are concerned, there is a lot of victim blaming these days. The assumption is that if you have been abused by a Bad Guy, it is your fault for not vetting them better, or for not escaping when you could.

It is rarely so simple.

Bad Guys might not be the majority, but they are all around us. Chances are you know several Bad Guys quite well. They are our family, friends, and coworkers. And not only are they great at what they do, but often we genuinely care for them.

It is easy for someone who has never been victimized to say, "You shouldn't have let it get so far." They were not there. They didn't see how slowly it progresses, how much love you can have for a Bad Guy, how much you can begin to depend on them.

So, once again, it is not your fault.

From now on, you have the necessary tools to identify Bad Guys and protect yourself. Anyone who would want to exploit you, hurt you, or just be consistently inconsiderate of your needs is much easier to see now. And that means that your life going forward should be largely free of such people and the harm they can do.

I wish you the best of luck in all your future relationships.

One last thing before you go – Can I ask you a favor? I need your help! If you like this book, could you please share your experience on Amazon and write an honest review? It will be just one minute for you (I will be happy even with one sentence!), but a GREAT help for me and definitely good Karma ☺. Since I'm not a well-established author and I don't have powerful people and big publishing companies supporting me, I read every single review and jump around with joy like a little kid every time my readers comment on my books and give me their honest feedback! If I was able to inspire you in any way, please let me know! It will also help me get my books in front of more people looking for new ideas and useful knowledge.

If you did not enjoy the book or had a problem with it, please don't hesitate to contact me at contact@mindfulnessforsuccess.com **and tell me how I can improve it to provide more value and more knowledge to my readers.** I'm constantly working on my books to make them better and more helpful.

Thank you and good luck! I believe in you and I wish you all the best on your new journey!

Your friend,

Ian

Don't hesitate to visit:
-My Blog: www.mindfulnessforsuccess.com
-My Facebook fanpage: https://www.facebook.com/mindfulnessforsuccess
-My Instagram profile: https://instagram.com/mindfulnessforsuccess
-My Amazon profile: amazon.com/author/iantuhovsky

If you haven't downloaded your free book already:

Discover How to Get Rid of Stress & Anxiety and Reach Inner Peace in 20 Days or Less!

To help speed up your personal transformation, I have prepared a special gift for you!

Download my full, 120-page e-book "Mindfulness Based Stress and Anxiety Management Tools" for free by clicking here.

Link:

tinyurl.com/mindfulnessgift

Hey there like-minded friends, let's get connected!

Don't hesitate to visit:

-My Blog: www.mindfulnessforsuccess.com

-My Facebook fanpage: https://www.facebook.com/mindfulnessforsuccess

-My Instagram profile: https://instagram.com/mindfulnessforsuccess

-My Amazon profile: amazon.com/author/iantuhovsky

Recommended Reading for You

If you are interested in Self-Development, Psychology, Emotional Intelligence, Social Dynamics, Soft Skills, Spirituality and related topics, you might be interested in previewing or downloading my other books:

Communication Skills Training: A Practical Guide to Improving Your Social Intelligence, Presentation, Persuasion and Public Speaking

Do You Know How To Communicate With People Effectively, Avoid Conflicts and Get What You Want From Life?

...It's not only about what you say, but also about WHEN, WHY and HOW you say it.

Do The Things You Usually Say Help You, Or Maybe Hold You Back?

Have you ever considered **how many times you intuitively felt that maybe you lost something important or crucial, simply because you unwittingly said or did something, which put somebody off?** Maybe it was a misfortunate word, bad formulation, inappropriate joke, forgotten name, huge misinterpretation, awkward conversation or a strange tone of your voice?
Maybe you assumed that you knew exactly what a particular concept meant for another person and you stopped asking questions?

Maybe you could not listen carefully or could not stay silent for a moment? **How many times have you wanted to achieve something, negotiate better terms, or ask for a promotion and failed miserably?**

It's time to put that to an end with the help of this book.

Lack of communication skills is exactly what ruins most peoples' lives.
If you don't know how to communicate properly, you are going to have problems both in your intimate and family relationships.

You are going to be ineffective in work and business situations. It's going to be troublesome managing employees or getting what you want from your boss or your clients on a daily basis. Overall, **effective communication is like an engine oil which makes your life run smoothly, getting you wherever you want to be.** There are very few areas in life in which you can succeed in the long run without this crucial skill.

What Will You Learn With This Book?

-What Are The **Most Common Communication Obstacles** Between People And How To Avoid Them
-How To Express Anger And Avoid Conflicts
-What Are **The Most 8 Important Questions You Should Ask Yourself** If You Want To Be An

Effective Communicator?
-**5 Most Basic and Crucial** Conversational Fixes
-How To Deal With Difficult and Toxic People
-Phrases to **Purge from Your Dictionary** (And What to Substitute Them With)
-The Subtle Art of **Giving and Receiving Feedback**
-Rapport, the **Art of Excellent Communication**
-How to Use Metaphors to **Communicate Better** And **Connect With People**
-What Metaprograms and Meta Models Are and How Exactly To Make Use of Them To **Become A Polished Communicator**
-How To Read Faces and **How to Effectively Predict Future Behaviors**
-How to Finally Start **Remembering Names**
-How to Have a Great Public Presentation
-How To Create Your Own **Unique Personality** in Business (and Everyday Life)
-Effective Networking

Direct link to Amazon Kindle Store: https://tinyurl.com/IanCommSkillsKindle

Paperback version on Createspace: http://tinyurl.com/iancommunicationpaperback

The Science of Effective Communication: Improve Your Social Skills and Small Talk, Develop Charisma and Learn How to Talk to Anyone

Discover the powerful way to transform your relationships with friends, loved ones, and even co-workers, with proven strategies that you can put to work immediately on improving the way you communicate with anyone in any environment.

From climbing the career ladder to making new friends, making the most of social situations, and even finding that special someone, communication is the powerful tool at your disposal to help you achieve the success you truly deserve.

In The Science of Effective Communication, you'll learn how to develop and polish that tool so that no matter who you are, where you go, or what you do, you'll make an impact on everyone you meet for all the right reasons.

Discover the Secrets Used By the World's Most Effective Communicators

We all know that one person who positively lights up any room they walk into, who seem to get on with everyone they meet and who lead a blessed life as a result.

Yet here's something you may not know:

Those people aren't blessed with a skill that is off-limits to the rest of us.

You too can learn the very same techniques used by everyone from Tony Robbins to Evan Carmichael to that one guy in your office who everyone loves and put them to work in getting what you want - without bulldozing over everyone in your path.

Step-by-Step Instructions to Supercharge Your Social Confidence

The Science of Effective Communication is a fascinating, practical guide to making communication your true super power, packed with expert advice and easy-to-follow instructions on how to:

- Retrain your brain to develop powerful listening skills that will help you build better relationships with anyone and gain more value from your conversations.
- Make your voice more attractive to potential romantic partners.
- Mend broken relationships with family members, partners, and even work colleagues.
- Get your views heard by those in authority without being disrespectful.
- Thrive in any job interview and get that dream job.

Your Complete Manual for Building Better Relationships With Everyone You Meet

Bursting with actionable steps you can use IMMEDIATELY to transform the way you communicate, this compelling, highly effective book serves as your comprehensive guide to better communication, revealing exclusive tips to help you:

- Overcome 'Outsider Syndrome,' make friends, and flourish in any social situation
- Keep conversations flowing with anyone
- Make long-distance relationships not only work, but positively prosper
- Reap huge rewards from a digital detox

And much, much more.

Direct Buy Link to Amazon Kindle Store: http://getbook.at/EffectiveCommunication

Paperback version on CreateSpace: http://getbook.at/EffectiveCommPaper

The Science of Interpersonal Relations: A Practical Guide to Building Healthy Relationships, Improving Your Soft Skills and Learning Effective Communication

From first dates and successful relationships to friends, colleagues, and new acquaintances, unlock the hidden secrets to successful communication with anyone and learn to flourish in any environment.

Guaranteed to change the way you think about relationships forever, The Science of Interpersonal Relations empowers you to identify those communication skills you need to work on and develop powerful techniques that will ensure your interpersonal relations thrive.

Your Complete Guide to Transforming Your Relationships

The Science of Interpersonal Relations is a book unlike any you've read before, not only in its approach to improving romantic relationships, but also on how to strengthen bonds and communicate better friends, family members, and even colleagues.

To really help you change your entire approach to communication, the book is split into two easy-to-read parts.

In part one, you'll change the way you think about the different relationships in your life and develop a whole new mindset that will lead you to healthy, positive, long-lasting relationships.

You'll discover:

- The real reason why so many relationships break down, and how to prevent yours from doing the same

- How to identify when you're being emotionally abused, and how to make it stop for good.

- Powerful solutions for dealing with negative people and protecting yourself against emotional vampires

- The secrets to successful assertiveness and the right way to say 'no' to anyone

- The links between personality styles and communication, and how to get the best out of any conversation with anyone.

In part two, you'll learn the tools and techniques you can put into action RIGHT NOW to start transforming your interpersonal relations for the better, including:

- Proven strategies for setting boundaries without hurting the other person

- The simple way for to help you meet your partner's real needs

- Effective techniques for identifying your partner's need for validation and providing it

and much more.

Discover the Real Reason You Don't Have the Relationship You Want - And What to Do About It

- Single and struggling to find that 'perfect' someone?

- In a relationship that you suspect might be in serious trouble?

- Dating someone you're convinced is 'The One' but not sure how to take that relationship to the next level?

Then this is the one book you can't live without.

Whatever situation you're in, single, dating, or struggling to keep that long-term relationship alive, you'll find simple-yet-effective instructions on how to create positive connections with the people in your life, including:
- How to determine what you really want in a relationship - and the red flags to watch out for that tell you someone really isn't right for you.
- How to turn heated arguments into positive experiences that help you and your loved one become closer and happier as a couple.

- How to identify if you're in a codependent relationship - and what to do about it.
- How to have "The Talk" about the state of your relationship and approach the subject of turning casual dating into something more serious.

Direct Buy Link to Amazon Kindle Store:

http://getbook.at/Relations

Paperback version on Createspace:

http://getbook.at/RelationsCS

Emotional Intelligence Training: A Practical Guide to Making Friends with Your Emotions and Raising Your EQ

Do you believe your life would be healthier, happier and even better, if you had more practical strategies to regulate your own emotions?

Most people agree with that.

Or, more importantly:

Do you believe you'd be healthier and happier if everyone who you live with had the strategies to regulate their emotions?

...Right?

The truth is not too many people actually realize what EQ is really all about and what causes its popularity to grow constantly.

Scientific research conducted by many American and European universities prove that the **"common" intelligence responses account for less than 20% of our life achievements and successes, while the other over 80% depends on emotional intelligence.** To put it roughly: **either you are emotionally intelligent, or you're doomed to mediocrity, at best.**

As opposed to the popular image, emotionally intelligent people are not the ones who react impulsively and spontaneously, or who act lively and fiery in all types of social environments.

Emotionally intelligent people are open to new experiences, can show feelings adequate to the situation, either good or bad, and find it easy to socialize with other people and establish new contacts. They handle stress well, say "no" easily, realistically assess the achievements of themselves or others and are not afraid of constructive criticism and taking calculated risks.

They are the people of success. Unfortunately, this perfect model of an emotionally intelligent person is extremely rare in our modern times.

Sadly, nowadays, **the amount of emotional problems in the world is increasing at an alarming rate.** We are getting richer, but less and less happy. Depression, suicide, relationship breakdowns, loneliness of choice, fear of closeness, addictions—this is clear evidence that we are getting increasingly worse when it comes to dealing with our emotions.

Emotional intelligence is a SKILL, and can be learned through constant practice and training, just like riding a bike or swimming!

This book is stuffed with lots of effective exercises, helpful info and practical ideas.

Every chapter covers different areas of emotional intelligence and shows you, **step by step**, what exactly you can do to **develop your EQ** and become the **better version of yourself**.

I will show you how freeing yourself from the domination of left-sided brain thinking can contribute to your inner transformation—**the emotional revolution that will help you redefine who you are and what you really want from life!**

In This Book I'll Show You:

- What Is Emotional Intelligence and What Does EQ Consist of?
- How to **Observe and Express** Your Emotions
- How to **Release Negative Emotions** and **Empower the Positive Ones**
- How to Deal with Your **Internal Dialogues**
- How to **Deal with the Past**
- **How to Forgive** Yourself and How to Forgive Others
- How to Free Yourself from **Other People's Opinions and Judgments**
- What Are "Submodalities" and How Exactly You Can Use Them to **Empower Yourself** and **Get Rid of Stress**
- The Nine Things You Need to **Stop Doing to Yourself**
- How to Examine Your Thoughts
- **Internal Conflicts** Troubleshooting Technique
- The Lost Art of Asking Yourself the Right Questions and **Discovering Your True Self!**
- How to Create Rich Visualizations
- LOTS of practical exercises from the mighty arsenal of psychology, family therapy, NLP etc.
- **And many, many more!**

Direct Buy Link to Amazon Kindle Store: https://tinyurl.com/IanEQTrainingKindle

Paperback version on Createspace: https://tinyurl.com/ianEQpaperback

Self-Discipline: Mental Toughness Mindset: Increase Your Grit and Focus to Become a Highly Productive (and Peaceful!) Person

This Mindset and Exercises Will Help You Build Everlasting Self-Discipline and Unbeatable Willpower

Imagine that you have this rare kind of power that enables you to maintain iron resolve, crystal clarity, and everyday focus to gradually realize all of your dreams by consistently ticking one goal after another off your to-do list.

Way too often, people and their minds don't really play in one team.

Wouldn't that be profoundly life-changing to utilize that power to make the best partners with your brain?

This rare kind of power is a mindset. The way you think, the way you perceive and handle both the world around you and your inner reality, will ultimately determine the quality of your life.

A single shift in your perception can trigger meaningful results.

Life can be tough. Whenever we turn, there are obstacles blocking our way. Some are caused by our environment, and some by ourselves. Yet, we all know people who are able to overcome them consistently, and, simply speaking, become successful. And stay there!

What really elevates a regular Joe or Jane to superhero status is the laser-sharp focus, perseverance, and the ability to keep on going when everyone else would have quit.
I have, for a long time, studied the lives of the most disciplined people on this planet. In this book, you are going to learn their secrets.

No matter if your goals are financial, sport, relationship, or habit-changing oriented, this book covers it all.

Today, I want to share with you the science-based insights and field-tested methods that have helped me, my friends, and my clients change their lives and become real-life go-getters.

Here are some of the things you will learn from this book:

• **What the "positive thinking trap" means,** and how exactly should you use the power of positivity to actually help yourself instead of holding yourself back?
• What truly makes us happy and how does that relate to success? Is it money? Social position? Friends, family? Health? **No. There's actually something bigger, deeper, and much more fundamental behind our happiness.** You will be surprised to find out what the factor that ultimately drives us and keeps us going is, and this discovery can greatly improve your life.
• **Why our Western perception of both happiness and success are fundamentally wrong**, and how those misperceptions can kill your chances of succeeding?
• **Why relying on willpower and motivation is a very bad idea, and what to hold on to instead?** This is as important as using only the best gasoline in a top-grade sports car. Fill its engine with a moped fuel and keep the engine oil level low, and it won't get far. Your mind is this sports car engine. I will show you where to get this quality fuel from.
• **You will learn what the common denominator of the most successful and disciplined people on this planet is** – Navy SEALS and other special forces, Shaolin monks, top performing CEOs and Athletes, they, in fact, have a lot in common. I studied their lives for a long time, and now, it's time to share this knowledge with you.
• Why your entire life can be viewed as a piece of training, and **what are the rules of this training?**

- What the XX-th century Russian Nobel-Prize winner and long-forgotten genius Japanese psychotherapist **can teach you about the importance of your emotions and utilizing them correctly in your quest to becoming a self-disciplined and a peaceful person?**

- How modern science can help you **overcome temptation and empower your will**, and why following strict and inconvenient diets or regimens can actually help you achieve your goals in the end?

- How can you win by failing and **why giving up on some of your goals can actually be a good thing?**

- How do we often become **our own biggest enemies** in achieving our goals and how to finally change it?

- How to **maintain** your success once you achieve it?

Direct Buy Link to Amazon Kindle Store: http://tinyurl.com/IanMentalToughness

Paperback version on Createspace: http://tinyurl.com/IanMTPaperback

Accelerated Learning: The Most Effective Techniques: How to Learn Fast, Improve Memory, Save Your Time and Be Successful

Unleash the awesome power of your brain to achieve your true potential, learn anything, and enjoy greater success than you ever thought possible.

Packed with proven methods that help you significantly improve your memory and develop simple-yet-powerful learning methods, Accelerated Learning: The Most Effective Techniques is the only brain training manual you'll ever need to master new skills, become an expert in any subject, and achieve your goals, whatever they may be.

Easy Step-by-Step Instructions Anyone Can Use Immediately

- Student preparing for crucial exams?

- Parent looking to better understand, encourage, and support your child's learning?

- Career professional hoping to develop new skills to land that dream job?

Whoever you are and whatever your reason for wanting to improve your memory, Accelerated Learning: The Most Effective Techniques will show you exactly how to do it with simple, actionable tasks that you can use to help you:

- Destroy your misconceptions that learning is difficult - leaving you free to fairly pursue your biggest passions.

- Stop procrastinating forever, eliminate distractions entirely, and supercharge your focus, no matter what the task at hand.

- Cut the amount of time it takes you to study effectively and enjoy more time away from your textbooks.

- Give yourself the best chance of success by creating your own optimal learning environment.

Everything you'll learn in this book can be implemented immediately regardless of your academic background, age, or circumstances, so no matter who you are, you can start changing your life for the better RIGHT NOW.

Take control of your future with life-changing learning skills.

Self-doubt is often one of the biggest barriers people face in realizing their full potential and enjoying true success.

In Accelerated Learning: The Most Effective Techniques, you'll not only find out how to overcome that self-doubt, but also how to thrive in any learning environment with scientifically-proven tools and techniques.

You'll also discover:
- How to use an ancient Roman method for flawless memorization of long speeches and complex information

- The secret to never forgetting anyone's name ever again.

- The easy way to learn an entirely new language, no matter how complex.

- The reason why flashcards, mind maps, and mnemonic devices haven't worked for you in the past - and how to change that.

- The simple speed-reading techniques you can use to absorb information faster.

- How to cut the amount of time it takes you to study effectively and enjoy more time away from your textbooks.

- The truth about binaural beats and whether they can help you focus.

- How to effectively cram any exam (in case of emergencies!).

And much more!

Direct Buy Link to Amazon Kindle Store:

http://getbook.at/AcceleratedLearning

Paperback version on Createspace:

http://getbook.at/AcceleratedLearningPaperback

Mindfulness: The Most Effective Techniques: Connect With Your Inner Self to Reach Your Goals Easily and Peacefully

Mindfulness is not about complicated and otherworldly woo-woo spiritual practices. It doesn't require you to be a part of any religion or a movement.

What mindfulness is about is living a good life (that's quite practical, right?), and this book is all about deepening your awareness, **getting to know yourself**, and developing attitudes and mental habits that will make you not only a successful and effective person in life, but a happy and wise one as well.

If you have ever wondered what the mysterious words "mindfulness" means and why would anyone bother, you have just found your (detailed) answer!

This book will provide you with actionable steps and valuable information, all in plain English, so all of your doubts will be soon gone.

In my experience, **nothing has proven as simple and yet effective and powerful as the daily practice of mindfulness.**

It has helped me become more decisive, disciplined, focused, calm, and just a happier person.

I can come as far as to say that mindfulness has transformed me into a success.

Now, it's your turn.
There's nothing to lose, and so much to win!

The payoff is nothing less than transforming your life into its true potential.

What you will learn from this book:

-What exactly does the word "mindfulness" mean, and why should it become an important word in your dictionary?

-How taking **as little as five minutes a day** to clear your mind might result in steering your life towards great success and becoming a much more fulfilled person? ...and **how the heck can you "clear your mind" exactly?**

-What are the **most interesting, effective, and not well-known mindfulness techniques for success** that I personally use to stay on the track and achieve my goals daily while feeling calm and relaxed?

-**Where to start** and how to slowly get into mindfulness to avoid unnecessary confusion?

-What are the **scientifically proven profits** of a daily mindfulness practice?

-**How to develop the so-called "Nonjudgmental Awareness"** to win with discouragement and negative thoughts, **stick to the practice** and keep becoming a more focused, calm, disciplined, and peaceful person on a daily basis?

-What are **the most common problems** experienced by practitioners of mindfulness and meditation, and how to overcome them?

-How to meditate and **just how easy** can it be?

-What are **the most common mistakes** people keep doing when trying to get into meditation and mindfulness? How to avoid them?

-**Real life tested steps** to apply mindfulness to everyday life to become happier and much more successful person?

-What is the relation between mindfulness and life success? How to use mindfulness to become much more effective in your life and achieve your goals much easier?

-**What to do in life** when just about everything seems to go wrong?

-How to become a **more patient and disciplined person**?

Stop existing and start living.
Start changing your life for the better today.

Amazon Kindle Store:

myBook.to/IanMindfulnessGuide

Paperback version on Createspace:

http://tinyurl.com/IanMindfulnessGuide

Buddhism: Beginner's Guide: Bring Peace and Happiness to Your Everyday Life

Buddhism is one of the most practical and simple belief systems on this planet, and it has greatly helped me on my way to become a better person in every aspect possible. In this book I will show you what happened and how it was.

No matter if you are totally green when it comes to Buddha's teachings or maybe you have already heard something about them—this book will help you systematize your knowledge and will inspire you to learn more and to take steps to make your life positively better!

I invite you to take this beautiful journey into the graceful and meaningful world of Buddhism with me today!

Direct link to Amazon Kindle Store: https://tinyurl.com/IanBuddhismGuide

Paperback version on Createspace: http://tinyurl.com/ianbuddhismpaperback

The Science of Self Talk: How to Increase Your Emotional Intelligence and Stop Getting in Your Own Way

We all speak to ourselves on a daily basis. Whether it's out loud or an internal (or infernal) commentary, we all practice self-talk and, how we speak to ourselves can have a significant effect on our emotions and subsequent actions.

Some people's self-talk is mostly about the future while, for others, it's an internal dialogue about the past. Some self-talk is positive and upbeat, while other self-talk is harsh, critical or defeatist.

Self-talk can focus on other people but, more often than not, it is about ourselves - and is often negative.

If you listen carefully, you'll notice that your inner conversation reflects thoughts and emotions. Self-talk isn't random. It exhibits patterns that repeat themselves. And everyone has their own characteristic self-talk that is uniquely theirs.

In The Science Of Self-Talk mindfulness expert, Ian Tuhovsky, explains how we can re-write the script when it comes to our internal communication. Through a series of simple exercises for use in daily life, you can understand your own self-talk in order to change the conversation.

Learn how you can listen to and understand your internal dialogue in order to change it.

Many of us practice negative self-talk by default - how many times have you called yourself an idiot or chastised yourself for not being good enough?

Negative self-talk is a harmful habit which can lead to anxiety, depression and helplessness and, yet, this is something that most of us do on a regular basis. For many people, this is learned behaviour whereby caution against boasting leads to self-criticism or self deprecation. For others, this is a natural reflection of the self and one that can slowly corrode self esteem.

This unique book covers:

- Constructive self-talk and dysfunctional self-talk - and knowing the difference.
- The impact of negative self-talk
- Learned helplessness

- Positive self-talk - challenge or threat?
- The Pareto Principle which says that, for many events, roughly 80% of the effects come from 20% of the causes.
- Creating the right circumstances for motivation
- Getting to know yourself
- Loving yourself - emotional intelligence
- Turning down the volume on your self-talk

In the past, people who engaged in negative self-talk or self-criticism were often labelled 'perfectionists', insinuating that it's actually a positive thing but it's so much more damaging than that.

Learning to identify our negative self-talk behaviour is the first step toward freeing us from its grip. With the right tools, we can change our internal dialogue, opening ourselves up to new opportunities, increased self-esteem and confidence.

More than just a self-help manual, The Science of Self-Talk is a Positive Psychology Coaching Series which explains the roots of self-talk, or, intrapersonal communication. The book explains that these are the thoughts that we 'hear' with the auditory part of our brain and which add a kind of commentary to our daily life.

Self talk is a little like turning on the director's commentary on a movie.

You can simply watch the movie or you can add in commentary about what's happening in it - this is, in a nutshell, what most of us do in our daily lives.

The Science Of Self Talk can help you to re-write the script of your movie and improve the way that you - and others - see yourself.

Direct link to Amazon Kindle Store: **mybook.to/IanSelfTalk**

About The Author

Author's blog: www.mindfulnessforsuccess.com

Author's Amazon profile: amazon.com/author/iantuhovsky

Instagram profile: https://instagram.com/mindfulnessforsuccess

Hi! I'm Ian...

. . . and I am interested in life. I am in the study of having an awesome and passionate life, which I believe is within the reach of practically everyone. I'm not a mentor or a guru. I'm just a guy who always knew there was more than we are told. I managed to turn my life around from way below my expectations to a really satisfying one, and now I want to share this fascinating journey with you so that you can do it, too.

I was born and raised somewhere in Eastern Europe, where Polar Bears eat people on the streets, we munch on snow instead of ice cream and there's only vodka instead of tap water, but since I make a living out of several different businesses, I move to a new country every couple of months. I also work as an HR consultant for various European companies.

I love self-development, traveling, recording music and providing value by helping others. I passionately read and write about social psychology, sociology, NLP, meditation, mindfulness, eastern philosophy, emotional intelligence, time management, communication skills and all of the topics related to conscious self-development and being the most awesome version of yourself.

Breathe. Relax. Feel that you're alive and smile. And never hesitate to contact me!

Made in the USA
Monee, IL
24 June 2023

36944126R00079